PUFFIN CLASSICS

Boyhood Days

Boyhood Days

RABINDRANATH TAGORE
Translated by Radha Chakravarty

Introduction by Amartya Sen

PUFFIN

PUFFIN BOOKS

Published by the Penguin Group

Penguin Books India Pvt. Ltd, 11 Community Centre, Panchsheel Park, New Delhi 110 017, India

Penguin Group (USA) Inc., 375 Hudson Street, New York, New York 10014, USA

Penguin Group (Canada), 90 Eglinton Avenue East, Suite 700, Toronto, Ontario, M4P 2Y3, Canada (a division of Pearson Penguin Canada Inc.)

Penguin Books Ltd, 80 Strand, London WC2R 0RL, England

Penguin Ireland, 25 St Stephen's Green, Dublin 2, Ireland (a division of Penguin Books Ltd)

Penguin Group (Australia), 250 Camberwell Road, Camberwell, Victoria 3124, Australia (a division of Pearson Australia Group Pty Ltd)

Penguin Group (NZ), 67 Apollo Drive, Rosedale, North Shore 0632, New Zealand (a division of Pearson New Zealand Ltd)

Penguin Group (South Africa) (Pty) Ltd, 24 Sturdee Avenue, Rosebank, Johannesburg 2196, South Africa

Penguin Books Ltd, Registered Offices: 80 Strand, London WC2R 0RL, England

First published in Bengali as *Chhelebela* in 1940
This translation first published in Puffin by Penguin Books India 2007

Translation copyright © Radha Chakravarty 2007

10 9 8 7 6 5 4 3 2

ISBN-13: 978-0-14333-021-9 ISBN-10: 0-14333-021-7

Typeset in Minion by Mantra Virtual Services, New Delhi
Printed at Pauls Press, New Delhi

This translation is dedicated to
Rohit, Kush and Kim

Contents

Introduction

This is an odd book. *Boyhood Days* is Rabindranath's own account of his early childhood, written by him at a ripe old age, shortly before his death. His recollections are invariably sharp, and yet, as Radha Chakravarty points out in her 'Translator's Note', not in all cases in line with those factual matters on which other evidence exists. And yet who better than Rabindranath himself to give us a glimpse of his life as a child? In fact, much the most interesting parts of this autobiography relate to his young mind: what the child Rabindranath thought, what ideas aroused the young boy, what he made of the world around him (his family, his city, his country, his globe), and what the school-age Rabindranath found sad in that world and in need of change—many of those diagnoses would stay with him through his entire life. On these matters there are no competing sources of real knowledge, and indeed the picture that we get from Tagore's recollections is both gripping in itself and deeply insightful in giving us an understanding of the adult man that would emerge from those boyhood days.

I am delighted, therefore, that a new translation and a fuller edition of this great book is now coming out as a Puffin Classic. Much has already been written about this book, based both on the Bengali original and the earlier translation by Marjorie Sykes (first serialized in *Visva Bharati Quarterly* and then published as a book in the same year, 1940). Obviously, Tagore's own account of his childhood days has intrinsic interest of its own, but it also tells us something about the development of the priorities that deeply influenced his later life. Of the many different connections that are of interest, let me select three for brief comments.

First, Rabindranath passionately disliked the schools he encountered, and as a dropout, he was educated at home, with the help of tutors. Already in his childhood he formed some views on what precisely was wrong with the schools he knew in the Calcutta of his day, some, as it happens, with fairly distinguished academic records. When Tagore established his own school in Shantiniketan (more commonly spelt as 'Santiniketan', but I shall follow here the translator's preferred spelling) in 1901, he was determined to make it critically different from the schools he knew. It is not always easy to spot what made his school, Shantiniketan, so different (this is in fact even more difficult to identify if you have been mainly schooled there, as I have been), but *Boyhood Days* tells a great deal about what Tagore was looking for in his vision of a school appropriate for children.

Sometimes a complete outsider can see things more clearly—and can explain more pithily—what is so special about an innovative institution than those engulfed in it can. The special qualities of the Shantiniketan school were caught with much clarity by Joe Marshall, a perceptive American trained at Harvard, who visited Shantiniketan in August 1914. He put it thus:

The principle of his method of teaching is that the individual must be absolutely free and happy in an environment where all is at peace and where the forces of nature are all in evidence; then there must be art, music, poetry, and learning in all its branches in the persons of the teachers; lessons are regular but not compulsory, the classes are held under the trees with the boys sitting at the feet of the teacher, and each student with his different talents and temperament is naturally drawn to the subjects for which he has aptitude and ability.[1]

All the points that caught Marshall's attention figure, in one way or other, in *Boyhood Days*—in the descriptions of what Tagore missed most in the schools he knew in his Calcutta.

Some of the things he missed and longed for, he actually did get at his own home, like the presence of music and poetry in everyday life. But he knew he was privileged and exceptionally fortunate, and he wanted to have schools where these facilities should come as standard part of the system, along with arrangements for academic training. I don't want to turn this Introduction into a 'Q & A' programme, but I will suggest to the reader, especially the young reader, that it

1. I am grateful to Megan Marshall, the distinguished author of the wonderful biography of the famous Peabody sisters, who 'ignited American romanticism' (*The Peabody Sisters*, Boston: Houghton Mifflin, 2005), for letting me see and draw on her grandfather Joe Marshall's unpublished 'Santiniketan journal'.

could be useful as well as fun to look for the connections that are plentifully there in Tagore's own account of his creative dissatisfaction about early education (not all the connections refer explicitly to schools at all—this is called, I believe, a 'hint' in 'help books').

One particularly important idea to look for is Tagore's focus on freedom, even for schoolchildren, on which Marshall did comment. This, in fact, identifies an aspect of Rabindranath that the standard commentaries on him— from W.B. Yeats and Ezra Pound onwards—missed. Yet his yearning for substantive freedom in human life comes through very clearly in *Boyhood Days*, and it stays throughout his life as a constant thought.[2]

Let me now turn to a second connection that deserves some attention. At his home Rabindranath was surrounded by people who loved music, varying in taste from austerely classical to more relaxed art forms of song-making and singing. Rabindranath had a fine introduction to classical Indian music, but he resisted the usual long years of formal training of the aspiring specialist. The range of Tagore's exposure and the choices he made profoundly influenced the development of his own musical genre, the astonishingly influential 'Rabindra-sangeet', still so very popular in Bangladesh and India.

---

2. I discussed this in my essay 'Tagore and His India', *New York Review of Books*, Vol. 44 (26 June 1997), republished in *The Argumentative Indian* (London and New Delhi: Penguin, 2005).

Kalpana Bardhan has commented on this connection between Rabindra-sangeet and Tagore's boyhood years in presenting her own translation of songs and commentaries on Tagore's work:

...Though he took some lessons, he resisted the systematic formal training his teachers insisted on. He imbibed freely from listening and impressed the grown ups by rendering what he heard. Surrounded by voice lessons and practice in classical singing, as he stopped going to school and stayed home, he went on constantly listening, humming to himself, nourishing his memory cells and vocal chords. In a way, as he liked to tell in his mature years, his boyhood resistance of a formal training in classical music, while gathering and absorbing it in his own way, freed him from the strictures of the Hindusthani classical music, and later on enabled him to intuitively blend raga melodies into mixed raginis for his songs, and further on to mix folk song tunes with classical melodies. The innovative mixings achieved the uniqueness of melody and lyric carrying each other in his songs, the balance of meaning through music and poetry.[3]

As we read through Tagore's account of his childhood years,

3. Kalpana Bardhan, unpublished manuscript. Earlier published as *Rabindranath Tagore's Songs of Love, Nature, and Devotion* (mimeographed, Berkeley, California, 2006).

we can find many scattered remarks on what would prove to be critically important preparation for the emergence of the wealthy tradition of Rabindra-sangeet.[4] *Boyhood Days* contains many glimpses—this is another 'hint'—of Rabindranath's exposure to the music around him which would ultimately help the birth of a new genre of Bengali music.

The third connection I want to comment on concerns Tagore's intellectual world, in particular the emergence of Tagore's rather special priorities in analytical and empirical inquiries and his expectations from them. This is a complex subject and has been much misunderstood. However, since the beginnings of Tagore's priorities and expectations are clearly noticeable in *Boyhood Days*, the subject deserves a little exploration here, for a better understanding even of the later Rabindranath.

Tagore's commitment to reasoning was strong—sometimes fierce—throughout his life. This is well reflected in his arguments, for example, with Mahatma Gandhi (whom he chastised for obscurantism), with religious parochialists (whose reasonless sectarianism upset him greatly), with the British establishment (for their crude treatment of India, in contrast with what he admired greatly in British intellectual life and creativity), with his Japanese admirers (who received, despite Tagore's general admiration of Japan, his sharply

---

4. A masterly account of the philosophical underpinnings of the tradition of Rabindra-sangeet can be found in Anisur Rahman's Bengali book, *Ashimer Spando*.

angry critique for their silence—or worse—in the face of Japan's newly-emerging supernationalism, including the Japanese treatment of China), and with the administrative leadership of both British India and the Soviet Union (he compared the Soviet achievements in school education across its Asian and European span very favourably with the gross neglect of school education in British India, while also chastising the Soviet leadership for its intolerance of criticism and of freedom of expression).[5]

Tagore's commitment to a reasoned understanding of the world around us came through also in his wholehearted support for scientific education (his school insisted on every child's exposure to the new findings emerging anywhere in the world). The same commitment to reason is seen also in Tagore's cultural evaluations, including his firm mixture of pride in Indian culture and rejection of any claim to the priority of Indian culture over all others. It is also seen in his refusal to see something called 'the Indian civilization' in isolation from influences coming from the rest of the world: this remains very relevant today, not just as a critique of what is now called the 'Hindutva' approach, but also of the widely popular theses of the 'clash of civilizations', which is frequently invoked these days as a gross—and rather dangerous—simplification of the complex world in which we live. In every case, Rabindranath's

---

5. More discussion of each of these issues can be found in my 'Tagore and His India'. See also, Krishna Dutta and Andrew Robinson, *Rabindranath Tagore: The Myriad-Minded Man* (New York: St. Martin's Press, 1996).

firm convictions were driven explicitly by critical reasoning which he clearly spelt out.

And yet to many contemporary observers in Europe and America, Rabindranath appeared to be anything but a follower of reason. It was faith he was identified with, and with a penchant for mystification over seeking clarity. While some of Tagore's admirers (of suitably mystical kind themselves) loved this 're-done Tagore', others found it unattractive, even detestable. A clear formulation of that interpretation of Tagore can be found in two unpublished letters of Bertrand Russell to Nimai Chatterji.[6] On 16 February 1963, Earl Russell wrote to Nimai Chatterji:

> I recall the meeting [with Tagore] of which Lowes Dickinson writes only vaguely. There was an earlier occasion, the first upon which I met Tagore, when he was brought to my home by Robert Trevelyan and Lowes Dickinson. I confess that his mystic air did not attract me and I recollect wishing he would be more direct. He had a soft, rather elusive, manner which led one to feel that straightforward exchange or

---

6. I am including, with Chatterji's permission, extracts from Russell's letter to him. Nimai Chatterji, a literary observer and critic, wrote to a great many people who knew Tagore asking them to comment on what they knew of—and thought of—Rabindranath, and this will form the corpus of a book on Tagore, we hope before very long (Chattterji's reluctance to publish his writings has been frustrating for his friends like me).

communication was something from which he would shy away. His intensity was impaired by his self-asorbtion [absorption]. Naturally, his mystic views were by way of dicta and it was not possible to reason about them.

In a later letter, dated 26 April 1967, Russell was even sharper in his denunciation of what he took to be Tagore's flight from reason:

His talk about the infinite is vague nonsense. The sort of language that is admired by many Indians unfortunately does not mean anything at all.

So what's going on here? Why would the reason-centred priorities of Tagore appear just the opposite of that to some towering intellectuals in Europe and America whom he met? And, in the present context, what insights can we get from Tagore's recollections in his *Boyhood Days* about this dissonance between Tagore's consistent championing of reason and Russell's belief that Tagore hated reason with a passion—a passion of the 'self-absorptive' kind. For an adequate understanding of what is happening, we have to take out, first, two incidental factors that no doubt had their influence but which could obscure a fuller picture of the contrasting intellectual priorities that lie behind the apparent dissonance.

The first incidental factor is Tagore's partial inclination to play the role that was assigned to him by his early admirers in England—W.B. Yeats, Ezra Pound and others—in which his poetical exposition, particularly in *Gitanjali*, of what can be seen as extraordinary features of the world overwhelmed his understanding of ordinary but very important things that make up the world and in which Tagore was (as *Boyhood Days* confirms) deeply interested from his very early days. This would later flower into his interest in science, culture, education, politics, ethics and epistemology. Russell 'knew' what to expect from the man that Lowes Dickinson brought to Russell's home, and he seemed to have decided that he got plentifully exactly what he expected to get from Rabindranath. Tagore's admirers in England would not leave much room for any way of contrasting the allegorical poetry of *Gitanjali* (itself over-mysticised by its English rendering) and Rabindranath's prosaic beliefs about the ordinary world. As I have discussed elsewhere, Rabindranath was initially happy enough to play this role, even though he was shocked by the over-praise he was getting.[7]

---

7. On the day after the famous literary evening of the reading of Tagore's poems in London that W.B. Yeats had arranged on 27 June 1912, he wrote to my grandfather, Kshiti Mohan Sen (who taught at Shantiniketan and later wrote, among other books, *Hinduism*, published by Penguin): 'Last night I dined with one of the poets here, Yeats. He read out the prose translations of some of my poems... People have taken to my work with such excessive enthusiasm that I cannot really accept it. My impression is that when a place from which nothing is expected somehow produces something, even an ordinary thing, people are amazed—that is the state of mind here.'

The second factor is Russell's propensity to dismiss anything that he did not find to be immediately clear to him. If Rabindranath got the raw end of that perspective in Russell's reactions to him, he did not fare any worse than Friedrich Nietzsche had in the caricature of him that Russell had produced in his *History of Western Philosophy*, in the form of a simulated conversation between Nietzsche and Buddha concocted by Russell to bring out the stupidity—as well as some possible nastiness—of Nietzsche's ideas as interpreted by Russell.[8]

Despite the importance of these factors, Rabindranath's understanding of intellectual priorities did, in fact, have some special features which contributed to the misunderstanding that is being examined. One of them was Tagore's willingness to accept that many questions will remain unresolved and their answers can remain incomplete. The domain of unfinished accounts would change over time, but not go away, and in this Rabindranath saw not a defeat but a humble—and also beautiful—recognition of our limited understanding of a vast world, even an incomprehensibly large, possibly infinite, universe (the kind of remark that so exasperated Russell). Rather than seeing this as a defeat of reason he clearly saw this as the way reason works in human life, at

---

8. Bertrand Russell's *History of Western Philosophy* was first published by Simon and Schuster in the USA, New York, in 1945.

any point of time.[9] He also saw some aesthetic beauty in the continuing incompleteness of our answers: this is where, I presume, Russell would have walked away had Tagore not been sitting at Russell's own home.

We can glimpse the early beginnings of this celebration of the unresolved and the incomplete in many remarks in *Boyhood Days* (this is another 'hint' to the young reader), but none perhaps more spectacular than the youthful Rabindranath's retreat from the discipline of tutored knowledge that was being poured into him. He would regain his peace when he could resume his reflection of the vast universe that lay beyond his tutors' grasp (p. 47):

In bed, at last, I found some moments of leisure. There, I listened to the story that never reached its conclusion: 'The prince rides across the boundless terrain...'

This is not the occasion to pursue Tagore's views of knowledge and reason further, and yet I found it striking, as I was rereading *Boyhood Days* (I had read the book, in Bengali,

---

9. Some features of Tagore's radical views of epistemology and objectivity played a big role in his much-reported conversation with Albert Einstein, on which see 'Einstein and Tagore Plumb the Truth', *The New York Times Magazine*, 10 August 1930. An attempt to understand Tagore's scientific position in terms of contemporary theories of realism (particularly Hilary Putnam, *The Many Faces of Realism*, Open Court, 1987) can be found in my essay, 'Tagore and His India'.

in my own boyhood days), how many of these connections with Tagore's epistemic and aesthetic priorities were already beginning to take shape in those early days.

Before ending, I would like to make a couple of comments on a more mundane subject. It has been claimed that to say goodbye is 'to die a little'. To read the translation of a book one knows in the original is also to die a little, and no translation, no matter how good and accurate, can prevent that.

One of the special problems arises in this case from the fact that words in one language sometimes do not have exact equivalents in another language. The problem is compounded by the fact that some words have more than one near-equivalent in another language. In fact, the English rendering of *Gitanjali*, somewhat influenced by Tagore's early admirers in England, had tended to select the most 'mystical' of the near-equivalents, sometimes mercilessly killing the necessary ambiguities in Tagore's Bengali expressions.

The plurality of near-equivalent English words applies even to the title of this book. 'Chhelebela'[10] in Bengali refers to childhood, even though the word used in that compound expression, to wit 'chhele', also does mean a boy, in its literal and original use. The Bengali language dropped gender about seven hundred years ago (there is not even any

---

10. Bengali sounds can be translated in different ways in English—a problem made more difficult by the fact that some Bengali sounds do not even exist in English! And here I am following the notation that the translator has chosen.

equivalent of the English distinction between 'he' and 'she', or between 'him' and 'her'), and it is quite standard for words like 'chhele' to be used to cover both sexes, that is, girls as well as boys. So 'chhelebela' could be translated as 'Childhood Days', and not specifically as 'Boyhood Days'. In this case, this might not matter tremendously, since Rabindranath was indubitably a man and his childhood was clearly his boyhood as well.

There is perhaps more of a problem with Tagore's 'Preface' which begins with the sentence: 'I received a request from Goswamiji to write something for the boys.' There were both boys and girls in the school (indeed my mother herself had been a student there long before me), and no matter what the genderized form of the Bengali expression is, Tagore's interest in presenting his recollections of his early years would have involved his willingness to cater to the curiosity of both boys and girls in the school (there is internal evidence of this in the text as well of Tagore's reach across the gender divide). Goswamiji too whose request, we learn from the Preface, started off this entire project, was a marvellous teacher, and as I remember vividly, cared no less for the girls than for the boys. The request for 'something for the boys' (taking the genderized form of words in the restrictive sense) must have included the girl students at the school as well. The coverage of many Bengali words, such as 'chhele', has this plasticity.

These uncertainties are, I suppose, inescapable in moving a book from one language to another. What is altogether remarkable is how much of the basic content of the Bengali original (including the atmosphere, the stories, the fears and the excitements, and Tagore's early reflections and analyses) have come through vividly and powerfully in this English version. I feel very privileged to have had the opportunity to introduce this fine translation of a remarkably engaging and stimulating memoir to the English-reading public. There is much to enjoy and learn from in this little book.

October 2006   Amartya Sen

Boyhood Days

Preface

I received a request from Goswamiji to write something for boys. Let me write about the young Rabindranath, I thought. I tried to enter that spectral world of the past. Its dimensions, internal and external, no longer correspond to the present-day world. Oil lamps, those days, emitted more smoke than light. The world of the mind had not yet been surveyed by science; the possible and the impossible were intertwined, the boundaries between them blurred. The language in which I have described those days is naturally easy, as suitable as possible for the minds of young boys. I have not changed my style while describing the stage when, with the passing of time, the naïve fancies of childhood began to clear like a fog from my mind; but the sense of those passages has crossed the limits of childhood. My account has not been allowed to breach the boundaries of childhood, but these recollections arrive, ultimately, at the threshold of adolescence. Pausing there, one can understand how a boy's psychology had evolved to maturity through an extraordinary convergence of accidental and inevitable circumstances. The special appropriateness of presenting this entire narrative as an account of one's 'boyhood days' lies in the fact that the growth of the child also signals the evolution of his spirit. In the early stages of life, it is this process that is primarily worth tracing. From his surroundings, this boy easily absorbed

3

the kind of sustenance that his spirit found congenial. The efforts to civilize him through conventional educational methods he accepted only in a limited measure.

Some features of this book's contents may be found also in *Jibonsmriti*, my memoirs, but that has a different flavour—like the contrast between a lake and a waterfall. That was a story, while this is birdsong; that belongs to the fruit basket, this to the tree, the fruits vividly visible among the surrounding branches and foliage. A while ago, like images captured on camera, some traces of this book had appeared in a book of verse. The book was called *Chhorar Chhobi*, 'Pictures in Rhyme'. The prattle in that book was part childish, part mature. The expressions of joy in it were largely of a whimsical, juvenile sort. In the present work, they assume the form of boyish prose.

Rabindranath Tagore

The Boy

I was then of tender age, and slight,
Like a wingless bird, my frame was ever so light.
From the neighbouring rooftop, pigeon flocks would rise
And crows on our balcony rails would utter raucous cries.
From across the street came the hawker's cry,
His gamchha-covered fish basket full of topshe fry.
There was Dada on the terrace, his vision fixed afar,
His violin tuned to the strains of the evening star.
Casting English books aside, to Boudidi we'd race,
A red-bordered sari framed her lovely face.
Hiding her keys in a flowerpot, like a prankster from hell,

I would try her temper, and test her love for me, as well.
Kishori Chatujje would arrive at nightfall,
In his left hand a hookah, on his shoulder a shawl.
The tale of Lav and Kush he would recite, at speed;
To my textbooks and notes I paid no more heed.
How I wished, that by whatever means at hand,
I could somehow join a minstrel band!
Travelling with my songs from place to place,
I wouldn't have a care about examinations to face.
When the schoolday was over, homewards I'd go,
And over our rooftop, I'd see the clouds hanging low.
In torrents of rain the street was sunk,
The pipes spouted water, like Airavat's trunk.
In the darkness, I listened to the music of the rain,
And thought of the prince, lost in a boundless terrain.
Of Kuyenloon, Mississippi and Yangtse Kiang I'd heard—
The mountains and rivers that in maps appeared.
The known, the half-known and the far-far-away,
Wove a web of many colours, so bright and gay!
A myriad movements, and sounds of myriad kinds,
In a flimsy universe, encircled by my mind.
Inside that world, my thoughts would lightly glide,
Like birds beneath a cloud, or flotsam on a tide.

Shantiniketan, Ashadh 1344*

*[Note: In the Bengali calendar this corresponds to the year 1937 of the Gregorian calendar.]

1

I was born in old-time Kolkata. Raising clouds of dust, hackney carriages would speed through the city, the horses' skeletal frames lashed by cord-whips. There were no trams, no buses, and no motorcars. Those days, life followed a leisurely pace, spared the breathless pressure of work. Having inhaled a stiff dose of tobacco, chewing paan, the babus would leave for office, some in palanquins or palkis, others in shared carriages. The well-to-do would ride carriages emblazoned with their family titles, the leather hoods overhead resembling half-drawn veils. In the coach-box rode the coachman, turban tilted at an angle, and at the back were two grooms, no less, yak-tail flywhisks swinging from their waistband, startling the pedestrians with their street-cry: '*Heinyo!*' Women, too shy to ride in carriages, ventured out in the stifling darkness of closed palkis. Never, in sunshine or in rain, would they shield their head with an umbrella. If a woman was seen wearing the long loose chemise or even shoes, she would be accused of aping the memsahibs, a sign of utter brazenness. If ever a woman came face to face with a man from another family, her veil would instantly descend over her countenance, down to the very tip of her nose, and she would turn her back on him, biting her tongue in shame. They went out in closed palkis, just as they lived behind closed doors at home. The wives and daughters of elite families would travel in palkis covered with an additional pall made of thick diamond-patterned linen. The palkis looked like walking graves. Accompanying the palki on foot would be a bodyguard, the darwanji, armed with a lathi. The darwans were supposed to remain stationed at the portico, guarding the main entrance to the house; to finger their beards; to deliver money to the bank and women to their paternal homes; and on auspicious days, to take the lady of the house for her holy dip in the Ganga, closed palki and all. When hawkers came to the door with their display-boxes, our darwan Shiunandan also received his share of the profits. And there was the driver of the hired carriage; if dissatisfied with the bakhra, or his share of the spoils, he would engage in a ferocious quarrel in front of the main gate.

Our pehelwan or strongman, sweeper Shobharam, would

from time to time contort his body to practice wrestling moves, exercise with heavy weights, pound hemp for his drink, or consume a horseradish, leaves and all, with great relish. We would go up close and scream 'Radhey-Krishna!' into his ear. The more he protested, throwing up his hands, the more stubbornly we persisted. This was his strategy for hearing us pronounce the names of his family deities.

The city, those days, had neither gas, nor electricity; when kerosene lamps appeared, we were amazed at their brilliance. At dusk, the attendant would go from room to room lighting castor-oil lamps. Our study was illuminated by a sej, a lamp with a double wick in a glass bowl.

In the dim, flickering light, our tutor, Mastermoshai, taught us the *First Book of Pyari Sarkar*. I would yawn, then become drowsy, and afterwards, rub my eyes to stay awake. I was repeatedly reminded that Mastermoshai's other pupil, Satin, was a gem of a boy, extraordinarily serious about his studies. He would rub snuff in his eyes to ward off sleep. As for me? The less said the better. Even the terrible prospect of remaining the only illiterate dunce among all the boys would not keep me alert. At nine in the evening, half-asleep, my eyes heavy with drowsiness, I would be set free.

The narrow passage from the public area to the inner quarters of the house was screened by venetian blinds, and lit by dim lanterns suspended above. Crossing it, I felt sure I was being followed. A shiver would run down my spine. Those days, you stumbled upon ghosts and spirits in stories and rumours, in the nooks and crannies of people's minds.

Every so often, the nasal wail of the shankchunni, the nocturnal spirit, would cause some maidservant to collapse in a fainting fit. That female ghost was the most temperamental of all, and she had a weakness for fish. There was also an unknown standing figure, straddling the dense almond tree to the west of the house, and the third floor cornice. There were many who claimed to have sighted that apparition, and no dearth of people who believed in the story. When my elder brother's friend laughed off the matter, the servants of the house were convinced that he knew nothing about religious faith. Just wait till the spirit wrung his neck one day, that would put an end to all his learned wisdom! Those days, the air was filled with terror, which had spread its net so wide that just to place one's feet under the table was enough to make one's flesh crawl.

There were no water taps, then. In the months of Magh and Phalgun, on bankhs or shoulder-borne yokes, bearers carried kolshis, rounded water pitchers filled with water from the Ganga. Inside a dark chamber on the ground floor, in row upon row of enormous water vessels, the year's supply of drinking water would be stored. It was a well-known fact that the spirits who secretly inhabited those damp, gloomy spaces on the lower floor, had huge, gaping mouths, eyes in their chests, ears like kulos—the flat U-shaped baskets used for husking puffed rice—and feet that faced the wrong way. As I crossed those ghostly shadows to reach the private garden of the house, my heart would heave in terror, adding wings to my feet.

Those days, at high tide, the waters of the Ganga would

flood the channels that lined the streets. From my grandfather's times, a share of those waters was reserved for our pond. When the sluices were opened, the foaming tide would descend like a waterfall, with a babbling sound. The fish would try to swim against the current. Clinging to the rails of the southern balcony, I would gaze at the scene in fascination. But the days of the pond were numbered. One day, cartloads of rubbish were thrown into it. As soon as the pond was filled up, it was as if the mirror reflecting the green shadows of the province had vanished. The almond tree remains, but there is no trace now of that ghostly spirit, though there is still space enough for him to straddle.

Now we have more light, both indoors and out.

2

The palki belongs to my grandmother's era. Its proportions are large and generous, cast in the royal mould. Each pole is designed for the shoulders of eight bearers. Gold bangles on their wrists, thick gold hoops on their ears, clad in red short-sleeved quilted jackets called mirjais, those bearers, with all the wealth and luxury of the bygone days, have faded away like the many-hued clouds of sunset. This palki was embellished with colourful designs, some of which have worn away. It is stained in places, the coir stuffing spilling out of the upholstery. Like a discarded item struck off from today's inventory, it lies abandoned in a corner of the veranda outside the khatanchikhana, the ledger-room. I was then about seven or eight. I had no useful role to play in this world; and that old palki, too, had been dismissed from all forms of useful employment. That was why I felt such a deep affinity with it. As if it was an island in the sea, and on holidays, I was Robinson Crusoe, lost to the world, concealed behind the palki's closed doors to elude the oppressive surveillance that surrounded me.

Those days, our house was full of people, and degrees of familiarity were not clearly demarcated. All around us was the hustle and bustle of male and female attendants deployed in different quarters of the household:

Pyari the maid, crossing the front yard, on her hip a dhama or large rattan basket laden with vegetables; Dukhan the bearer, fetching water from the Ganga in pitchers suspended from the bankh balanced on his shoulder; the weaver-woman, making for the inner quarters of the house, to peddle saris designed with the latest borders; Dinu the salaried goldsmith who served our family, pumping the hissing bellows in the room beside the alley, heading for the ledger-room to claim his payment from Kailash Mukhujje, the man with the quill pen tucked behind his ear; in the courtyard, the dhunuri, fluffing the cotton stuffing of old quilts, to the clanging sound of his bow-shaped cotton-gin. And outside, the doorman Mukundalal, rolling about on the ground, practising wrestling grips with the blind pehelwan, noisily slapping his thighs before performing twenty or twenty-five push-ups in quick succession. And a

13

crowd of beggars waiting, hoping for their regular portion of charity.

As time advanced, the sunlight grew harsh, the bell in the portico announced the time; but inside the palki, the day refused to keep track of the passing hours. In there, it was the noontime of those bygone days, when the danka, the large kettledrum at the palace gate, would signal the end of the public audience, and the king would depart for his daily bath in sandalwood-scented water. One afternoon, on a holiday, my supervisors had dozed off after their daytime meal. I was alone. The immobile palki sped through the terrain of my mind, borne by loyal minions made of air. The path they traversed had been carved out from my own whims and fancies. On that route the palki travelled, to faraway lands bearing names gleaned from books. Sometimes, the journey would take the palki into deep forests, where tiger eyes gleamed, and the flesh crept in fear. With me was hunter Biswanath. *Bang!* went his gun, and it was all over. All was still.

Then, at some other point, the palki transformed into a mayurpankhi, a magical boat shaped like a peacock. It floated on the ocean, no sign of land anywhere. In regular rhythm, the oar hit the water, *splash! splash! splash!* Up and down, swaying and heaving, the waves rose and fell. 'Watch out! Watch out! Storm ahoy!' cried the sailors. At the helm was oarsman Abdul, with his pointed beard, shaven upper lip, and bald pate. I knew him. From the river Padma, he fetched tortoise eggs and hilsa fish for Dada, my elder brother.

He told me a story once. One day late in the month of

Chaitra, he was out fishing in his dinghy when there was a sudden summer thunderstorm, a kalboishakhi. It was a terrible storm; the boat was about to sink. Gripping the tow rope with his teeth, Abdul dived into the water and swam to the sandbank, tugging the boat ashore.

I did not like a story that ended so quickly. The boat didn't even sink, and he survived so easily—this was no story at all!

'What happened next?' I kept prodding him.

'What a to-do there was, then!' he replied. 'I found myself face-to-face with a wolf. What enormous whiskers he had! During the storm, he had climbed onto the pakur tree on the other shore, near the market. A gust of wind, and the tree fell into the Padma. Our friend the wolf was adrift in the rushing torrent. Gasping for air, he reached the sandbank and clambered ashore. As soon as I saw him, I wound my rope into a noose. The creature confronted me with the glare of his huge, bulging eyes. All that swimming had whetted his appetite. The sight of me made his bright-red tongue begin to water. He knew many folks inside out, but he didn't know Abdul. "Come, my little one!" I called out. The moment he reared up on his hind legs, I flung the noose round his neck. The harder he struggled to free himself, the tighter the noose became, making his tongue hang out.'

'Did he die, then, Abdul?' I enquired anxiously, at this point.

'No power on earth could allow him to die!' Abdul assured me. 'With the river in flood, I had to get back to Bahadurganj, didn't I? Tying him to the dinghy, I got the wolf cub to tow the boat a distance of at least twenty crosh—about ten miles. He moaned and groaned, I prodded his belly with the oar, and in an hour and a half, he'd covered the distance of a ten-to-fifteen-hour journey. Don't ask what happened next, baba, for you will not get a reply!'

'Very well,' I agreed, 'so much for the wolf. Now, tell me about the crocodile?'

'I've often seen the tip of his nose jutting out above the water,' replied Abdul. 'Stretched out on the sloping river-shore, basking in the sun, he seems to have a hideous smile on his face. With a gun, I could take him on. But my license had expired. A funny thing happened, though. One day, Kanchi bedeni the snake-catcher was scraping split bamboo with the curved blade of her da, her baby goat tethered by her side. Sneaking up from the river, the crocodile grabbed the baby goat by the leg and began to drag it away, towards the water. In a single leap, the bedeni was astride the crocodile's back. Using her da, she struck blow upon blow on that giant reptile's neck. Relinquishing the baby goat, the creature sank into the water.'

'And then?' I cried, in agitation.

'Reports of what happened next have sunk to the bottom of the river,' replied Abdul. 'It will take a long time to retrieve the information. I shall send a scout to find out what happened, and bring you the details when we meet again.'

But he hasn't come back since. Perhaps he has gone to find out what happened.

So much for my travels within the palki. Outside the palki, I sometimes played the schoolmaster, with the veranda railings for pupils. They were silent with awe. There would be the occasional naughty ones, not interested in lessons at all. They would grow up to be coolies, I would warn them. Beaten black and blue, they would still show no sign of giving up their pranks. It wouldn't do to let the mischief end, after all: for that would put an end to my game.

There was one more game I played, with Singhimama, my wooden lion. Tales of animal sacrifices performed on prayer days had convinced me that sacrificing my lion would be an event of great magnitude. Many were the blows I rained upon his neck with a twig. I had to make up the mantra, of course, for no puja is complete without that:

Singhimama, off with your head!
At Andibose's shrine I strike you dead!
Ulkut dhulkut dum dum dum
Walnut balnut whack-whack-whack
Crack-crack-crack!

Almost all the words here were borrowed. Only 'walnut' was my own. I had a weakness for walnuts. From the word 'whack', it will be apparent that my scimitar was made of wood. And 'crack' suggests that the scimitar was none too strong.

3

Since last night, the clouds have not played truant. It has rained without pause. The trees seem numb and stupefied. The birds have fallen silent. Today, I remember the evenings I spent as a child.

We passed our evenings in the quarters occupied by our domestic staff. Our evenings were not yet burdened with the terrifying, heart-stopping task of memorizing the spelling and meaning of English words. The brickwork of Bangla must be in place before an overlay of English could be applied, as Sejdada, the third of my elder brothers, would say. That is why, when schoolchildren of our age were fluently chanting

'I am up' and 'He is down', my own learning had still not advanced beyond 'b-a-d bad, m-a-d mad'.

In the aristocratic parlance of those times, the staff quarters were referred to as the toshakhana or treasury. Although our standard of living had declined to a level far beneath that of the old-world elite, names like toshakhana, daftarkhana for office, and baithakkhana for the sitting-room, still clung to the foundations of our home.

Inside a large chamber at the southern end of that toshakhana, a dim light burned in a glass sej filled with castor oil. A painting of Ganesha and a palm-leaf hanging inscribed with the image of Kali adorned the walls, and around the pictures, geckoes lay in wait for insect prey. The room was bare of furnishings, with only a dirty mat on the floor.

Let me inform my reader that our lifestyle was humble. We rarely used horse-drawn carriages. Outside the house, in one corner, a palki and an old horse were kept inside a shed beneath the tamarind tree. The clothes we wore were extremely ordinary. It took a long time for us to graduate to wearing socks. When bread and banana-leaf-wrapped pats of butter were assigned for our evening snack in violation of the scanty menu usually prescribed for us by our servant Brajeswar, it seemed that heaven was within our reach. We were being trained to adapt easily to the disintegration of old-world splendour.

The attendant in charge of our gatherings on the floor-mat was a man called Brajeswar, with salt-and-pepper hair and moustache, taut dry skin stretched over his face, a severe disposition, a harsh voice, and a guttural accent. His previous employer was Lakshmimanta, a person of eminence. From that position, he had been forced to descend to the job of minding carelessly-brought-up children like us. I had heard that he was formerly a schoolmaster in the village pathshala. He still retained the language and mannerisms of a schoolteacher. Instead of saying, 'The babus are waiting,' he would say, 'They are expecting you.' The masters of the house would laugh at the way he spoke. His fetish for cleanliness matched his self-esteem. When bathing, he would step into the pond and push away the oily surface scum several times before plunging his head into the water. Emerging from the pond after his bath, Brajeswar would stride along the garden path, arms held out at an angle, as if to preserve his caste purity by somehow evading this filthy world in which destiny had placed him. He would elaborate, with great emphasis, on what was proper or improper in matters of deportment. The tilt of his head added authority to his words. All the same, there was a flaw in his schoolmasterly behaviour. Deep within, he nursed a craving for food. It was not his habit to offer us full servings on our platters at mealtimes. When we sat down to eat, he would wave a luchi casually before us, and ask, 'Do you want some more?' His tone would indicate the answer he wanted. 'I don't want any,' I would often reply. After that, he would not press me to have more. He also had an uncontrollable attraction for the milk bowl, a taste I did not share at all. On the shelves of a cupboard inside his room were a large brass bowl of milk, and luchi with cooked vegetables on a wooden tray. Outside the cupboard's wire-mesh doors, you could feel the presence of a catlike greed, circling the spot, sniffing the air.

In this way, I had grown quite accustomed to frugal meals, right from my boyhood days. I can't claim that these sparse meals had made me weak. I was as strong as the boys who ate without restraint, if not stronger. My health was so disgustingly sound that even when I longed restlessly to play truant from school, I could not make myself ill by abusing my body in any way. I would roam all day with my shoes soaked in water, without catching a cold. In the cold month of Kartik, I would sleep on the open terrace, my hair and clothes growing damp, without experiencing the faintest irritation of the throat that might signal the beginning of a cough. And I never felt the symptoms of indigestion that manifest themselves in stomach ache, though I would complain of the condition to my mother. Ma would listen to me in secret amusement, without appearing worried in the least. All the same, she would summon the attendant and instruct him, 'Very well, go and tell the tutor that he can take the day off.'

Our old-fashioned mother would see no harm in her son missing an occasional lesson. Had I fallen into the hands of today's mothers, I would not only have been sent back to the tutor, but had my ears tweaked as well; or perhaps, with a suppressed smile, she would have made me swallow castor oil, to cure my illness forever. Sometimes, on a rare occasion, I would develop a high temperature, but nobody would call it a fever, describing it merely as body heat. Doctor Nilmadhav would come by. I hadn't set my eyes upon a thermometer, then; touching me briefly, the doctor would prescribe fasting and castor oil for the first day. I was allowed a little water to drink, and tepid water at that with a flavouring of cardamom. By the third day, a diet of mourola fish in gravy, served with sticky, overcooked rice, tasted like heavenly nectar after all the fasting.

I don't remember having ever suffered a prolonged fever. Malaria was a foreign word. Castor oil was the most nauseating medicine I ever took, but I have no memory of quinine. My skin never felt the touch of a scalpel used to lacerate a boil. To this day, measles and chicken pox remain unknown to me. My body was stubbornly healthy.

Mothers who wish to keep their sons disease free so they can't elude their tutors, should find attendants like Brajeswar. For such caregivers will reduce expenditure on food bills, and on doctors' bills as well, especially in these days of mill-ground flour and adulterated ghee and cooking oil. We must remember that chocolate had not yet appeared in the market. Instead, there was pink revri, available for one paisa. Whether this sesame-encrusted, rose-flavoured lump of sugar still makes boys' pockets sticky, I cannot say; it must have fled in embarrassment from the homes of today's elite. Where has it gone, that paper bag full of fried masala? And the goja, that cheap sesame-flavoured sweet? Have these things survived? If they haven't it is best not to revive them.

In instalments, every evening, I heard Brajeswar recite

the seven-canto Bengali Ramayana composed by Krittivasa. In the midst of those readings, Kishori Chatujje would appear. He knew the entire panchali, or musical folk-style Ramayana by heart, chanting tunes and all. All of a sudden, he would seize the limelight, overriding Krittivasa with his fluent recitation of the panchali couplets, 'O Lakshman, look, what evil signs! What dangers beset us now!' With beaming countenance and glistening bald pate, he would let the doggerel verses flow from his throat like a musical waterfall, the rhymes at the end of each couplet resonating like pebbles in the current. He would punctuate the performance with vivid gestures to illustrate the verses' meaning.

It was Kishori Chatujje's greatest regret that Dadabhai— yours truly, that is—could not join a panchali troupe, despite my musical talent. Given the opportunity, I could have made a name for myself in my own region, at least.

When it grew dark, the floor-mat assembly would disperse. Bowed down by my terror of ghosts, I would head for my mother's room. Ma would then be playing cards with her khuri, or paternal aunt. The room with its patterned parquet floor gleamed like ivory, the enormous bedstead covered with an embroidered, quilted spread. I would make such a nuisance of myself that she would fling down her hand of cards and exclaim, 'What a troublesome boy! Go, Khuri, tell them a story.' Having washed our feet in the outer veranda with water from a ghoti, we would climb into bed, dragging our great-aunt with us. There, we would embark upon the adventure of awakening the princess from her slumber, to rescue her from the giant's castle. Halfway through the story, no power on earth could have awakened me from my slumber! During the wee hours, the call of the jackal could be heard. Those days, the howling of jackals could still make that old house in Kolkata shudder, down to its very foundations.

4

When we were young, the city of Kolkata was not as wide awake in the evening as it is now. Today, electric lights take over as soon as the hours of daylight end. At that time, the city had less work, but no rest—like embers that continue to smoulder after the fire in the stove has died down. The oil-press has stopped, the steamer siren is silent, the labourers have trooped out of the factories, the buffaloes yoked to jute-laden carts have retired to their tin-roofed shelters in the city. But the nerves of the city seem to be throbbing still, inflamed by their daylong struggle with problems of all kinds. In the shops that line the street on both sides, it is business as usual, only a little subdued, like embers beneath ashes. Motorcars groan in many voices, rushing in all directions, but there is not much urgency behind their speed.

In those olden times, at the day's end, it was as if all pending tasks had curled up under a dark blanket and quietly gone to sleep in the city's unlit nether regions. The gloom of dusk hung heavy, indoors and out. From the street, one could hear the grooms call out as their carriages returned from the Ganga shore at Eden Gardens, where they had taken pleasure-seekers on a joyride. 'Barif!' the hawkers on the streets would shout, in the hot months of Chaitra and Baisakh. Inside a handi filled with salted ice-chilled water were tiny tin cones containing what was then called kulfi, now known as ice or ice cream. How those cries stirred my heart as I stood on the veranda facing the street, only my heart can tell. 'Belphul!'—jasmine—was another street cry.

Today, there is no trace of those gardeners with their springtime flower baskets. I wonder why. Those days, the air was full of fragrance, wafting from the belphul garlands adorning the braided hair-knots of the women of the house. Before their evening bath, the women, sitting outside their rooms, would gaze into hand-held mirrors as they braided their hair. The plaits would be twisted into elaborate hair-knots in various intricate styles. The women would be dressed in black-bordered Pharashdanga saris, draped with twisted pleats. The barber's wife would arrive to scrub their feet with a jhama, before applying alta, or the red lac-dye. Women like her were the gossip mongers in the female quarters.

Those days, on their way home from college or office, people would not crowd the entrance steps of trams, in a rush to reach the football field. They would not collect in hordes in front of cinema halls. There was a certain enthusiasm about theatre, but—what can I say?—we were very young, those days!

Boys, those days, could take no part in adult pleasures, even from a distance. 'Go away, go and play!' we would be told, if we plucked up the courage to go anywhere near. But if boys played boisterously, as they should, they would be admonished. 'Be silent!' they would be told. Not that adult entertainment was always conducted silently. From a distance, every now and then, some snatches of it would be flung our way, like frothing foam from a waterfall. Leaning over the balcony, I would observe the scene, gazing at the dance-hall of the house opposite, sparkling with light. Outside the portico, enormous horse-drawn carriages would drive up. Some of our elder brothers would welcome the guests and escort them upstairs. They sprinkled rose water from the nozzled spray called a golap-paash, and handed out tiny posies. From time to time, the sobbing of some high-caste kulin girl in the play would waft to my ears, but the meaning of those sobs eluded me. I had a terrible urge to know. The 'girl' who wept was of pure caste, no doubt, for I was told 'she' was really my brother-in-law playing a female role. In our family, those days, the worlds of men and women were poles apart, and so were the worlds of adults and children. In the chandelier-lit baithakkhana, the song-and-dance routine would be in progress; the elders would be puffing away at their gurguris; the women, with their caskets of paan, would be concealed in the dimness behind the jharokhas, windows with ornate filigree screens. Other women would assemble there as well, and in whispered tones, exchange news of what went on in their households. The boys would be in bed. Pyari or Shankari would be telling us a story, the words drifting into my ears:

Like moonlit blossoms . . .

5

A little before our time, in the households of the rich, amateur jatra, or popular theatre performances, had come into vogue. It was the custom to select shrill-voiced boys for the troupe. Mejokaka, the second of my father's younger brothers, led one such amateur group. He had a talent for composing dialogues in musical rhyme, and the enthusiasm to train the boys. If these amateur theatricals flourished in wealthy homes, professional jatra was also very popular, all over Bengal. Jatra troupes would mushroom in every other neighbourhood, under the banner of some eminent theatre personality or other. Not that the owners of these theatre groups were distinguished in caste or education. They had earned plaudits by their own efforts. In our house, there would be occasional jatra performances. But they were out of bounds for me, because I was young. I glimpsed the preparations for the performances. The troupe would take over the veranda, the entire area enveloped in tobacco smoke. The lads were long haired with dark shadows under their eyes, faces prematurely aged, lips stained from incessant paan chewing. In painted tin boxes, they carried their costumes. Through the open entrance door at the portico, a teeming mass of people surged into the courtyard. The noise boiled over and spread in every direction, spilling beyond the alleyway into Chitpur road. At about nine o'clock at night, like a hawk swooping down on a dove, Shyam would suddenly appear. 'Ma has sent for you. Come to bed!' he would order, grasping my elbow in his hard, calloused fist. Embarrassed at being dragged off in public, I would admit defeat and head for the bedroom. Outside, there was hustle and bustle, the sparkle of chandeliers. In my room, there was no noise at all; the brass lamp burned dimly on its stand. In the depths of my slumber, I could hear the clash of cymbals every time the taal, the rhythm-cycle of the dance, reached the point of climax called the sam.

Adults consider it their sacred duty to forbid everything. But on one occasion, they unbent for no apparent reason, decreeing that even the boys would be allowed at the jatra performance. The performance was based on the legend of Nal and Damayanti. Before the show commenced, I remained asleep in bed until eleven at night. We were repeatedly assured that we would be awakened as soon as it was time. Knowing the ways of those in authority, it was hard to believe their promises. For they were grown-ups, and we were children.

That night, I dragged my reluctant body to bed. For one thing, my mother had assured me that she herself would wake me up. Besides, it took considerable effort to keep myself awake after nine. At some point, I was awakened and led outside. My eyes were dazzled. On the ground floor and the floor above, sparkling lights shone forth from coloured chandeliers; swathed in white sheets, the courtyard looked enormous. At one end sat the masters of the house and invited guests. The rest of the space was filled by all and sundry. The performance had drawn an audience of eminent persons, gold chains hanging from their waists, and at this jatra performance, adults and children sat cheek by jowl. Most of the people at the gathering consisted of what civilized persons would describe as 'riff raff'. But then, the lyrics for the musical dialogues had been composed by provincial scribes who had learned to write with pens made of reed, and not from English copy-books. The music, dance and narratives that made up this show were born of Bengali soil; the language had not been polished by the pundit moshais who taught at village schools.

When we joined our elder brothers at the gathering, we were handed small amounts of money knotted into handkerchiefs. It was customary to fling the money at the performers at appropriate moments, to applaud the performance. This brought extra earnings to the jatra troupe, and a good reputation to the host.

Night drew to a close, but the jatra showed no signs of ending. I had no idea when my limp body was carried away from the scene. Had I sensed what was happening, it would have been no mean embarrassment for someone who watched the show with adults, flinging tips at the performers! When I woke up, I found myself on my mother's bed. The day was far advanced, the sun shining brightly. For the sun to have risen while I was still in bed—such a thing had never happened before!

Nowadays, in the city, pleasure flows like a stream. There are no intermittent breaks in its flow. Every day, at any odd hour, there are cinema shows; at a minimal cost, anyone may gain entry at will. Those days, a jatra performance was like probing for water in the sands of a dry river-bed at intervals of several miles. It would last for a few hours, quenching the thirst of passers-by who dropped by at random to have their fill.

Those bygone days were like a prince, dispensing largesse occasionally, at their pleasure, at auspicious moments, in their own areas of jurisdiction. These present days are like merchants' sons, displaying all sorts of glittering wares at the crossroads, to attract buyers from the highway, and from the alleyways as well.

6

Brajeswar was head of our domestic staff. Next in command was a person called Shyam. A pure provincial hailing from Jessore, he did not speak the language of Kolkata; he would use his local dialect, saying *tenara* and *onara* instead of *tara* and *ora* for 'them' and 'they,' *khati hobe* and *jati hobe* instead of *khetey hobey* and *jetey hobey* ('we must eat', 'we must go'), *mugir* dal and *kulir ambol* for moong dal and jujube chutney. 'Domani' was his term of endearment for us. Shyam was dark complexioned, with large eyes, long, oil-drenched locks, and a sturdy, well-built physique. Harshness was alien to his nature, and he was simple of heart. He had a

33

soft corner for us young boys. From him, we would get to hear stories about dacoits. Those days, tales of robbery circulated in every household, just as the fear of ghosts pervaded people's minds. Not that robberies are scarce now. Murder, assault with injury, loot and plunder, all these crimes continue to take place even now, and the police, too, continue to arrest the wrong persons. But all this is mere news; it lacks the spice of a story. Tales of bandits, those days, would crystallize slowly, evolving through hearsay over a long period of time. When we were very young, you could still find men who had belonged to bandit gangs in their prime. Big-built lathi-wielders they were, accompanied by their disciples, apprentices to the art of fencing with staves. People would salaam at the very mention of their names. Robberies, those days, were seldom randomly violent and bloody. They were acts of daring that displayed largeness of heart. Meanwhile, even in the homes of the gentry or bhadralok, training schools had mushroomed to promote the skill of fencing with lathis. Ustads, masters of the art, were acknowledged even by the dacoits, who avoided their terrain. Many zamindars made robbery their trade. I heard a story about one member of this fraternity, who had stationed his gang at the river's estuary. It was a moonless night, a holy occasion. After performing a ritual human sacrifice for the skull-adorned Goddess Kali, when they brought the severed head to the temple, the zamindar struck his forehead in grief. 'But this is my own son-in-law!' he cried.

Even more popular were the tales of Bandit Raghu and

Bandit Bishu. Not for them the ways of the lowly and ignoble: before committing a robbery, they would warn their prospective victims in advance. When their blood-curdling rallying cry was heard from afar, the entire locality would cower in terror. Their faith forbade them to touch women. Once, a woman disguised as Kali, brandishing a scimitar, had turned the tables on them, forcing the dacoits to pay her a devotional offering.

A display of banditry skills was organized at our house, once. They were huge, dark-skinned youths, all of them, with long, flowing hair. Tying up the rice-husking pedal in a sheet, they gripped the cloth between their teeth, and flung the dhenki over their shoulder. Tethering people to the ends of their shaggy hair, they swung them round and round. They vaulted to the first floor on their long staves, and flew, bird-like, through the gap between a person's outstretched hands. They also showed us how, after committing a robbery ten or fifteen miles away, one could return home the same night and lie innocently in bed. Bits of wood tied crossways, halfway down tall wooden stilts, would serve as footholds. These stilts were called ronpas. Holding the upper ends of the ronpas, feet secure on the footholds, one could move faster than a horse, a single stride covering the distance of ten normal steps. Though I did not have robbery in mind, I had once urged the boys at Shantiniketan to get used to walking on ronpas. How many evenings have I spent as a child, clutching my sides in terror, the image of this display of banditry merging, in my mind's eye, with the tales told by Shyam!

It was Sunday, a holiday. The previous evening, as crickets chirped in the thickets of the garden to the south, we had been listening to the story of Bandit Raghu. Inside the room, with shadows flickering in the dim light, my heart was pounding. The next morning, taking advantage of the holiday, I ensconced myself in the palki. Motionlessly, it began to move, heading for an imaginary destination, so my mind, still caught in the magic web of last night's story, savoured the thrill of danger. The pulse of the darkness beat in rhythm with the palanquin bearers' chants—*Hanyi-hunyi! Hanyi-hunyi!* Fear made my flesh creep. The field stretched into the distance, the air quivered in the sunlight. Far away, one could see the glinting water of the oblong pond Kalidighi, and the glitter of sand. At the shore, the pakur tree, branches outspread, bent low over the cracked and fissured ghat.

The fantasy conjured up an atmosphere of dread, which hung over the cane thickets beneath the trees on that unfamiliar field. I advanced, my heart trembling in fear. Projecting above the thicket, the tips of several bamboo staves could be seen. The palki bearers were to change position at this point. They would have a drink of water, and wrap damp gamchhas round their heads. And then? We would hear the bandits' rallying cry!

'*Re re re re re re re!*'

7

From dawn to dusk, the mill of education ground on. My Sejdada Hemendranath, the third of my elder brothers, was in charge of operating this machine. He was a hard taskmaster. If stretched too tight, the strings of the tanpura snap with a twang. There is no denying, now, that most of the excess baggage with which he had tried to overload our minds has sunk without trace like the cargo of a capsized boat. My education must be written off as a dead loss.

Sejdada was busy grooming his daughter. At the appropriate time, he admitted her to Loreto House. Even before that, she had acquired first-language proficiency in

Bengali. He honed Protibha's skills in Western music. As we knew, this had not diverted her from her pursuit of desi music. No member of the gentry, those days, could match her at Hindustani music. The advantage of Western music is that it trains the ear through intensive practice of musical scales, and the rigour of piano playing also does not permit slackness of rhythm. Meanwhile, she had been learning Hindustani music from Bishnu, from her very infancy. I, too, had to join this training school. Today's musicians, famous or obscure, would scoff at the songs with which Bishnu initiated me into the realm of melody. For they were the humblest forms of local doggerel. Let me offer a few examples:

A gypsy lass once came our way,
And charmed us with the tattoo's art,
In patterns after our own heart.
What magic in those tattoos lay,
O sister-in-law, my Thakurjhi!

But the tattoo's sting, it made us smart,
And how we wept, O Thakurjhi!

I remember a few more fragments, such as:

Sun and moon admit defeat,
The firefly shines so bright.
The Mughals and Pathans retreat,
And the weaver reads Persian with delight.

Do not plague the plantain tree,
Your daughter-in-law, just let her be,
O Ganesh's Ma! You know
If a single plantain-flower should grow,
How many little 'uns there will be!

One can even recall lines that retain the flavour of old, forgotten news:

There was a thicket of thorns, all overgrown,
A jungle fit for dogs alone;
They chopped it up to build a throne.

Today, it is customary to begin by rehearsing the notes—sa re ga ma—to the accompaniment of the harmonium, before introducing the pupil to light Hindi songs. But the person who monitored our education those days had realized that childishness is congenial to young boys' natures, and that this colloquial form of Bengali would win their hearts more readily than the Hindi language. Besides, these indigenous measures dance to the natural beat of the pulse, oblivious of the bol—the formal rhythmic chant—of tabla and bayan. Infants are first introduced to the magic of literature through the lines of doggerel recited by their mothers, and initiated into the magic of music through these same rhymed verses. These truths were demonstrated through the experiments to which we were subjected.

The harmonium had not yet appeared on the scene to

corrupt the purity of our regional music. I rehearsed my songs with the tanpura resting on my shoulder, not enslaved by musical notes produced through the mechanical pressing of keys.

In the pursuit of knowledge, nothing held my attention for long: this was my weakness. I filled my bag of learning with pickings from here and there, as the fancy took me. If diligent pursuit of learning had come naturally to me, the ustads of today would not have taken my work so lightly.

I had plenty of opportunity. As long as Sejdada was in charge of our education, I absent-mindedly parroted devotional songs, Brahmosangeet, for Bishnu. Sometimes, when my heart was spontaneously drawn to the music, I picked up songs from listening at the door. Sejdada would rehearse *Atigajagamini re*, and from my place of hiding, my heart would absorb the imprint of that music. It was very easy to astonish my mother by singing the same song to her in the evening.

Srikantha babu, our family friend, immersed himself in melody, day and night. He would massage his body with chameli oil on the veranda before his bath. From his hand-held gurguri, the fragrance of damp tobacco would waft to the sky, and his continuous humming would cast a spell on all the boys in the vicinity. But he never gave lessons; music was his gift, which we received, unawares. When his ecstasy got the better of him, he would rise to his feet, dancing as he played upon his sitar, his enormous eyes shining with delight, and sing:

He would insist that I sing along with him.

Those were the days of open-door hospitality. Degrees of acquaintance, or regular contact, did not matter much. Anyone who came, at any time, would be offered a bed to sleep in, and the customary dish of rice. Such an unknown guest once arrived, his tanpura balanced on his hip. Settling down, legs outstretched, at one end of the sitting room, he undid his bundle of belongings. Kanai, the tobacco-attendant, handed him a hookah as a matter of course. Guests, those days, would be entertained with paan as well as tobacco. In the private quarters of the house, it was the women's morning chore to prepare heaps of paan for the visitors who frequented the outer chambers. Swiftly, they would smear the betel leaf with chuna or lime-paste, add khoyer—catechu—with a stick, stuff the paan with spices, roll it up and fix it with a clove, and add it to the heap inside the deep brass bowl covered with a damp, khoyer-stained rag. Meanwhile, in the chamber beneath the staircase, the tobacco ritual would be in full swing. Ash-covered roasted tobacco was placed in earthenware basins, the nozzles of the albola, or hookah's flexible tubes, dangling like the serpent demons of the snake-filled netherworld, Nagaloka, their nerves steeped in the fragrance of rose water. Visitors to the house, as they approached the stairs, were greeted first by the welcoming scent of this damp amburi tobacco. It was the rule, in those days, to accept all human beings into the

41

household. That bowl of paan, full to the brim, has long since vanished. And the hookah-attendants have shed their livery. They now spend their days in the sweet shop, kneading three-days-old sandesh to a paste.

That unknown singer remained with us for a few days, at his own will. Nobody asked any questions. At dawn, I would drag him from under the cover of his mosquito net, to hear him sing. Those without a talent for routine learning take a fancy to unstructured education. In the tunes meant for morning hours, he would sing: *Bangshi hamari re.*

Then, when I was a little older, a major ustad Jadubhatta ensconced himself in our house. He made a big mistake, for he insisted on training me in music. That is why I never learned music at all. I garnered a few things in secret. I enjoyed *Rum jhum barakhe aaju badarawa* in raga Kafi; to this day, it has remained closely associated with my rain songs.

To complicate matters, another guest arrived unannounced at the same time. He was a renowned tiger killer. As it seemed quite extraordinary, those days, for a Bengali to be a tiger slayer, I remained riveted to his room most of the time. He had not really been bitten by a tiger, as he claimed in the tale that left us wonderstruck; the story of the tiger bite was fabricated from his vision of the open-mouthed dead tiger in the museum. This did not occur to me then, but now I understand clearly. At the time, in any case, I had to busy myself sustaining a frequent supply of tobacco for this hero. From a distance, the strains of alaap in raga Kanhra would waft to my ears.

So much for music. Under Sejdada's supervision, the foundations of my education in other branches of learning were also broad-based. That they did not bear much fruit is due to the flaws in my nature. It was with people like me in mind that Ramprasad Sen had declared: 'O my heart, you do not understand what cultivation is all about.' I had never taken to cultivation.

Now for an account of the fields of learning in which the plough of education had tried to make some furrows.

I left my bed when it was still dark, and donned my wrestler's garb; in winter I would shiver, and get goosebumps on my skin. We were trained by a redoubtable muscleman from the city, named Kana Pehelwan—the blind wrestler. To the north of the hall was an empty stretch of land, known as the golabari or granary. From the name which had survived, it will be apparent that there was a time when the city had not entirely engulfed the provincial areas; there were still some gaps and loopholes. In the early days of urban civilization, our golabari would store a year's supply of grain. The tenant farmers on our land would give us a portion of their rice crop. Against the golabari wall was the thatched shed for wrestling. The soil was dug up and loosened to a depth of about a foot and a half, and a maund of mustard oil poured into it, to prepare the pitch. There, practising wrestling grips with the pehelwan was a mere game for me. When I was thoroughly smeared with grime, I would eventually dress and depart. My mother was not pleased at the thought of my muddying myself so freely every morning, fearing that her son would acquire a soiled complexion. Therefore, on holidays, she would try to undo the damage. Nowadays, fashionable housewives purchase jars of skin-whiteners from shops peddling foreign merchandise; but those days, they would prepare the ointments themselves. The applications would contain ground almonds, cream, orange-peel, and all sorts of things. Had I known and remembered the ingredients, I could have sold the product under the brand name 'Begumbilash'—'My Lady's Delight'—and earned profits that would put a sandesh shop to shame. On Sunday mornings, I would be subjected to a thorough scrubbing in the veranda. My heart would yearn for release. Meanwhile, the rumour persisted, among the boys at school, that infants in our family were dipped in alcohol at birth, to add a foreign gloss to our complexion.

Returning from the wrestling ring, I would find a student from the medical college waiting to teach me all about human bones. Suspended on the wall was a complete human skeleton. There it hung, on our bedroom wall at night, the bones rattling in the breeze. After handling the bones and learning all their difficult names, I lost my fear of them.

The bell in the portico announced seven o'clock. Tutor Nilkamal arrived on the dot, there was no question of a minute's delay. He had a thin, emaciated body, but his health, like his pupil's, never failed, not once did he complain of a headache. I would go up to the table, books and slate in hand. On the blackboard, chalk marks, all in Bengali, would inscribe the mathematical signs of arithmetic, geometry, algebra. In literature, I had graduated directly from *Sitar Banabas* to *Meghnadbadh Kabya*. Alongside, I also read *Prakrita Bigyan*, a textbook of natural science. Sometimes, my teacher Sitanath Dutta, would pay us a visit, and we would get a faint whiff of the latest scientific news by verifying what we already knew.

Once, we received a visit from Heramba Tatvaratna. I began to learn the Sanskrit grammar book *Mugdabodh* by heart, without understanding a word of it. The heavier the daylong pressure of learning a variety of subjects, the harder my mind would endeavour to secretly discard some of the weight. The knowledge learned by rote would struggle for loopholes to escape the net, and tutor Nilkamal's opinion of his pupil's calibre was not worth announcing to all and sundry.

At the other end of the veranda sat the old tailor with his flint-glass spectacles, bent over his sewing, taking occasional breaks to pray at the appointed times. Observing Neyamat, I would marvel at his happy life. When my head spun from doing too many sums, I would shield my eyes with my slate and glance down at Chandrabhan in front of the portico, as he plied a kankoi, a thick-toothed comb, to part his beard, drawing up the ends and tucking them behind his ears. Beside him, the slim young doorman shredded tobacco, wearing an ornamental wristband called a kankon. At the same spot, the horse had consumed his customary bucketful of grain, and the crows hopped about, pecking at the scattered chickpeas. Johnny the dog dutifully woke up to give them chase, barking loudly.

In the dust heap swept into the corner of the veranda, I had planted a wood-apple seed. My heart was restless with anticipation, waiting for it to sprout. As soon as my tutor Nilkamal left, I felt compelled to run and check on the seed, and to water it. Ultimately, my hopes remained unfulfilled. The heap of dust was swept away by the same broom that had once brought it into being.

The sun climbed the sky, casting half the courtyard in shade. Nine o'clock. Short, dark-skinned Gobindo, dirty yellow gamchha on his shoulder, would escort me to my bath. Sharp at nine-thirty, we were served our fixed portions of the routine menu: dal, rice and machher jhol, fish cooked in gravy. I had no taste for it.

The bell announced ten o'clock. From the highway came the distracting call of the hawker peddling unripe mangoes. Far off, the clinks and clanks of the utensil-seller could be heard, as he travelled even further away. On the terrace of the house at the end of the alley, the eldest daughter-in-law of the family dried her damp hair in the sun; her two daughters played with cowries, unmindful of the time. Girls did not have to hurry to school, those days. It seemed so fortunate to be born a girl! The old horse would haul me in the palki carriage to my own Andamans, my place of exile from ten to four. I would return from school after four-thirty. My gymnastics trainer would have arrived by then. For about an hour, I would swivel around a wooden bar. As soon as he left, my art teacher would appear.

Gradually, as the rusty daylight waned, the blurred,

miscellaneous sounds of the city would lend a dream-like musical quality to that giant body made of bricks-and-scaffolding.

In the study, oil lamps were lit. Tutor Aghor made his appearance. The English lesson commenced. The reader, with its dark jacket, seemed to crouch on the table, waiting to pounce. The cover was loose, the pages torn and stained; in the wrong places, I had honed my writing skills, inscribing my name in English, all in capital letters. As I read, I dozed off; every now and then, I would start into wakefulness. The time I spent not reading far exceeded the hours I devoted to studying.

In bed, at last, I found some moments of leisure. There, I listened to the story that never reached its conclusion:

'The prince rides across the boundless terrain. . .'

8

I clearly sense the difference between those days and our present times when I notice that neither humans nor ghosts and spirits frequent the rooftops of today's dwellings. As I have mentioned earlier, the Brahmadaitya has fled, unable to survive in an atmosphere of excessive bookishness. Gone are the rumours about the demon relaxing with his leg propped up on the cornice of our terrace. That space is now full of crows fighting over mango seeds sucked dry and discarded. Meanwhile, beneath the roof, human habitation is confined to square-walled rooms that resemble packing cases.

I remember the walled terrace of the interior portion of our house. In the evening, Ma would spread a floor-mat of woven reed, and chat with the female companions who surrounded her. Their talk required no hard facts. Their only need was to while away their time. Those days, there was no regular supply of diverse pastimes to fill the hours of the day. The day was not a close-knit mesh, but more like a loose net with spacious gaps and openings. At male gatherings as well as women's get-togethers, the gossip and banter was very light-hearted. Chief among Ma's companions was Brojo Acharji's sister, popularly known as Acharjini. In this circle, she was the conduit for daily gossip. She would usually arrive loaded with morsels of extraordinary news, garnered or invented. These would incite the women to dwell upon the expensive rituals that must be performed in order to maintain domestic peace. Before this circle I would sometimes display my learning, freshly gleaned from textbooks. The sun was ten million miles away from the earth, I would tell them. From *Rijupath Part 2*, I recited a chunk of *Valmiki Ramayana*, no less, Sanskrit diction and all. Ma had no way of gauging the accuracy of her son's pronunciation, but the brilliance of his learning extended along the sun's ten-million-mile-long trajectory to dazzle her, all the same. Who would have thought that such shlokas could be recited by anyone other than Sage Narada?

This terrace, above the private quarters of the house, belonged entirely to women. The place was well in tune with the demands of the larder. It received the direct sunlight, which facilitated the pickling of lemons. There, the women, their brass vessels full of ground black gram, squeezed out drops of the mixture to form baris, while they dried their hair in the open. The female attendants would hang out the washing in the sun. Strips of unripe mango were dried to make amshi, and mango juice was poured into stacked-up black-stone ornate moulds of diverse sizes, and left to congeal. Tender jackfruit pickle, steeped in mustard oil, would mature in the sun. Keya-khoyer, screwpine-scented catechu, was prepared with great care. That is something I have special reason to remember. When my schoolteacher informed me that he had heard of the keya-khoyer prepared at my house, his meaning was not hard to understand. What he had heard about, he must experience. Hence, to sustain my family reputation, I would sometimes go up to the terrace, to plunder—why say steal?—a few pieces of keya-khoyer. For even kings and emperors resort to plunder when necessary—or even when not necessary—while condemning those who steal to prison, or even to death by impalement. It was the women's duty to chase away crows as they whiled away their time, chatting on the terrace in the mild winter sunlight. As the only deor or younger brother-in-law in the house, I was deployed to guard Boudidi's aam-papad made of dried and flattened mango pulp. I was also her companion in sundry other minor household tasks. I would read to her from *Bangadhipa Parajaya*. Sometimes, I would be given the task of shredding supari or betel nut, with the chopper called a janti. I could chop supari very fine. Bouthakrun would never acknowledge any of my other talents; she would even fault my appearance until I cursed my fate. But she had no hesitation in exaggerating my prowess when it came to shredding supari. So, my supari-chopping proceeded at a brisk pace. In the absence of an enthusiastic audience, I have long since applied my fine supari-shredding skills to other delicate pursuits.

In these feminine chores that filled the terrace, there was a flavour of the provincial. These tasks belonged to an age when the house had space for the dhenki or rice-pedal, when coconut was shredded to make the sweetmeat called naru, when the maidservants rolled lamp wicks on their thighs in the evening, when neighbours would invite us for a ritual meal on the eighth day after a child was born. These days, boys don't listen to fairy tales narrated by women; they read the stories in print, all by themselves. We must now buy pickles and chutneys from New Market, bottled in corked containers sealed with lac.

The chandimandap, the pavilion for the worship of Goddess Durga, also bore a rustic stamp. Gurumoshai, as the schoolmaster was called, ran the pathshala there. The boys of our family, and our neighbours' sons as well, began their education there, making scratch marks on palm-leaf parchment. I, too, must have scrawled my first letters of the alphabet at that very place, but like the remotest planet of the firmament, that infant image remains beyond the range of memory's telescope.

My earliest memories of book learning are of the accounts

of the monstrous events at Sage Shandamarka's pathshala, and of Narasimha, the divine incarnation, savaging Hiranyakashipu's abdomen. Probably, I even saw a lead engraving of that scene, in my book. And I recall some fragments of Chanakya's shlokas.

In my life, that open terrace was the main area of freedom. On that terrace, from infancy to adulthood, I passed my days—all sorts of days, spent in all sorts of ways. When my father was home, he would occupy the room on the second floor. Concealed behind the attic, I would often watch him from afar, as he meditated silently before sunrise, hands folded on his lap, like a white stone statue on the terrace. Sometimes, he would depart for the hills, and be away for many days. Then, visiting that terrace gave me the thrill of high adventure, like crossing the seven seas. Through the gaps in the veranda railings downstairs, I had observed the movements of people in the street; but to climb up to the terrace was to transcend the boundaries of human habitation. Once there, my imagination would stride across the rooftops of the city, to the place where the blue of the sky merged with the green of the earth. The rooftops, high and low, belonging to buildings of diverse shapes, caught the eye; in the gaps between them, one could see the shaggy heads of trees. I would often steal up to the terrace in the afternoon. Afternoon is a time of day that has always captivated my heart. It is the resting period, like the night-time of the daylight hours, when the boy–hermit renounces the world. Sliding my hand through the shutter slats, I would unlatch the door to the bedroom. Directly facing the door was a sofa; where I would ensconce myself, feeling utterly alone. The watchmen authorized to hold me captive were drowsy, their stomachs full; stretching and yawning, they lay sprawled across their floor-mats.

The rays of the sun acquired a rosy hue, kites soared in the sky, calling loudly. The bangle-seller traversed the alley in front of our house, calling out his wares. Gone, today, is the hush of those afternoons, gone the hawkers who frequented those hours of silence. Their sudden call would reach the ears of the bride of the house, as she lay in bed, open tresses outspread on her pillow. The maidservant would escort the old bangle-seller into the house, where he would press and squeeze, easing the clear glass bangles of her choice onto his client's tender wrists. Today, the bride of those days will not yet have attained the status of a wife: she will still be learning second-grade lessons by rote. And the bangle-seller of yore will perhaps be plying a rickshaw on that very same alley. The terrace, for me, was the desert I had read of in books, its bleak desolation stretching in every direction, the hot breeze stirring up a cloud of dust, as the blue of the sky grew dim.

In the desert that was the terrace, an oasis had appeared. These days, the water-supply does not reach the taps on the upper stories of the house. But those days, the water reached even the rooms on the second floor. The bathroom with its concealed entry was like a new discovery for this infant Livingstone of Bengal. I would turn on the faucet, and the running water would splash all over my body. Drying my body with a bed sheet, I would feel very relaxed.

In no time at all, my period of leisure would be over. The bell in the portico announced four o'clock. On a Sunday evening, the sky seemed to grimace hideously. The shadow of Monday's approaching eclipse had already begun to swallow the evening in its open mouth. Downstairs, by now, they would be searching for the boy who had eluded his captors.

It was time for the evening snack. This was Brajeswar's red-letter hour. It was his charge to shop for our snack. Those days, shopkeepers did not make a profit of thirty to forty per cent on the price of ghee, and the snacks they sold had not yet acquired a poisonous taste and smell. If we were lucky enough to receive kachauri or singara, or even aloo dum, it did not take us long to consume it. But, at the appointed hour, when Brajeswar would cock his already-arched neck and say, 'Look, Babu, see what I have brought today,' we would usually find fried peanuts in a paper bag. Not that we did not fancy peanuts, but his dignity rested on his parsimony. We never made the faintest sound of protest. Not even on the days when teele-goja, the sesame-flavoured sweetmeat, emerged from its palm-leaf packaging.

The daylight was waning. With a heavy heart, I managed to circle the terrace; glancing downwards, I saw that the ducks had left the pond. There was activity at the ghat, the waterfront, where people had begun to move to and fro as the shadow of the peepal tree lengthened, stretching across half the pond. From the street came the call of the coachman, driving a judigadi, a coach and pair.

9

Days passed by in this monotonous fashion. School would gouge out a large chunk of the day, the remaining hours scattered across the morning and afternoon. As soon as I entered the classroom, the tables and benches would seem to prod my mind with their dry, angular elbows. Day after day, they looked as stiff as ever. I would return home at dusk. In the study, the oil lamp shone like a signal directing me to prepare my lessons for the following day.

Once in a while, the man with the dancing bear would visit our courtyard. Or the snake charmer, to make his snakes perform. Sometimes, to add a touch of novelty, the street magician would appear. On our Chitpur road, one can no longer hear the sound of the dugdugi, their small tabor. They have fled the land, those people, bowing out to make way for the cinema, saluting it from afar. Like the breed of grasshopper that blends its hue with the colour of dry leaves, my heart, too, would wear a faded tint, to merge with the dryness of those days.

Very few games were available to us, those days. We could play marbles, or what was known as batball—a very distant cousin of cricket. And we could spin tops, or fly kites. All the games played by boys in the city were of this type, demanding no hardiness. Football, which required players to bound across the entire field, seemed ocean leagues away from our lives. And so my days, all of exactly the same measure, confined me in a circular maze of dry fence posts.

Then one day, the notes of the shehnai rang out in Baroan tones. Into the house came a new bride, thin gold bangles on her tender dark wrists. In the blink of an eye, a gap opened up in the fence, to reveal a newcomer from magic lands beyond the boundaries of our familiar world. I circled her from afar, afraid to come close. She had assumed a position of importance, while I was just a negligible youngster.

The house was then divided into two separate quarters, known as mahals. The men occupied the outer portion, while the women remained in the inner chambers. The style of the nawabs was still in vogue. I remember Didi, my elder sister, strolling on the terrace with the new bride, exchanging intimacies. When I tried to get close, she sent me packing with a rebuke. This area was out of bounds for boys. I must return, crestfallen, to the shadow of those dingy old days of routine existence.

When from far-off hills the rain-floods descend, they swiftly undermine the foundations of ancient dams. So it was with us, now. The lady of the house declared the advent of a new dispensation. Bouthakrun was allotted the room adjoining the private terrace. The terrace became her domain. Wedding feasts for dolls were held there, leaf platters and all. This youngster—yours truly—would be the guest of honour at such celebrations. Bouthakrun was a good cook, and an excellent hostess; she found me a willing guest to satisfy her taste for entertaining. As soon as I returned home from school, I would be offered food she had herself prepared, sanctified by her touch. And on days when she mashed chorchori, mixed vegetables prepared with shrimp, into the panta bhat or fermented rice with a light flavouring of chilli, there was no containing my delight. Sometimes, when she was away visiting relatives, I would be enraged to find her sandals missing from their place outside her door, and would hide some precious item from her room, to force a quarrel.

'Who's supposed to mind your room when you are away?' I would feel compelled to argue. 'Am I your chowkidar, your minder?'

'You need not mind my room,' she would retort angrily. 'Just mind your thieving hands.'

Women of today would find this ridiculous. Was there never a deor in any household save yours, they might ask. I acknowledge the truth of what they say. Nowadays, people seem suddenly more mature, in every respect, than those who belonged to those earlier times. Those days, everyone, old or young, was youthful at heart.

Here began a new chapter of my lonely, nomadic existence on the terrace, for into my life came human companionship, and human affection. It was my elder brother, Jyotidada, who held centre stage at this point.

10

A fresh breeze was blowing in the kingdom of the terrace, a new season had arrived. Our esteemed father had left the Jorasanko House, by then. Jyotidada took up residence in the room on the second floor. In a corner of that room, I carved a tiny niche for myself.

The veil that screened the andarmahal, the inner quarters, was lifted. Today, this would not seem unfamiliar, but at that time, the idea was so new that there was no yardstick by which to gauge its novelty. Long before that, when I was an infant, Mejdada, the second of my elder brothers, had returned to the country as a civilian. When he set out for

Bombay to join work, he shocked outsiders by taking his wife, my Bouthakrun, with him, right before their very eyes. It was bad enough that he should have carried his wife away to far-off foreign lands instead of leaving her behind with the family; but to make no attempt to shield her from public view en route signalled an outrageous disregard for convention. Our own kith and kin were devastated, as if the sky had collapsed on their heads.

Women had still not grown used to public attire at that time. Bouthakrun was the first to adopt the sari-and-blouse combination fashionable today. Young girls then had not yet taken to wearing frocks, tossing their braided hair—not in our household, at least. It was customary for the young ones to wear the long dress called the peshwaj. Bordidi, my eldest sister, was very young when the Bethune School was founded. There, she was among the pioneers of easy access to education for girls. Her complexion was extraordinarily fair. In our part of the world, she was beyond compare. Once, dressed in a peshwaj, on her way to school in the palanquin, she was waylaid by the police, who mistook her for an abducted English girl—so we heard.

As I have mentioned before, there was an unbridgeable communication gap between adults and children, those days. But, in the tangled world of those old customs, Jyotidada had arrived, with a mind pure and untainted. I was twelve years his junior. It was amazing that I should attract his notice, despite this vast difference in age. More surprising still was the fact that he never silenced me by rebuking my precocity during our interchanges. Hence, I never lacked the courage to give my thoughts free rein. Today, it is in the company of young boys that I live. I raise various issues for discussion, but find them silent. They hesitate to ask questions. I realize that they belong to the old order where adults spoke, while youngsters remained mute. Young people of the new age have the courage to ask questions, while youngsters trapped in the age of adult domination accept everything in silence, with bowed heads.

In the room on the terrace, a piano appeared. And furniture from Bou Bazaar, burnished in the modern style. Our chests swelled in pride. In the gaze of the once-impoverished, the arrogance of the nouveau riche appeared.

The fountain of my music now began to play. Running his fingers over the piano keys, Jyotidada composed rhythmic melodies in ever-new styles. He would keep me beside him. It was my task to provide an instant supply of words to accompany those racy tunes, holding the notes in place.

At the end of the day, mats and bolsters would be arranged on the terrace. On a silver dish, jasmine garlands wrapped in damp handkerchiefs would be placed, there would be a tumbler of iced water on a saucer, and in a bowl, fragrant paan of the indigenous variety. Freshly bathed and dressed, her hair coiffed, Bouthakrun would take her place. Jyotidada would appear, a light wrap cast airily across his shoulders. He would put his bow to the violin, and I would launch into song on a high note. The Creator has never taken away the slight talent for music he had granted me. Across the rooftops my song would carry, and into the sunset sky. From the far-off sea, the southern breeze would blow, and the sky would fill with stars.

Bouthakrun had transformed the terrace into a regular garden, with rows of tall palms on the balustrades, surrounded by flowering plants: chameli, gandharaj, rajnigandha, karabi, dolonchampa. It did not occur to her that this might damage the terrace; we were a whimsical lot, all of us.

Akshay Chowdhury was a frequent visitor. That he was tone deaf was a fact he knew well, and others knew even better. But there was no stemming the tide of his song. He was especially partial to the Ragini Bihag. He sang with his eyes closed, blind to the facial expressions of his listeners. If he laid his hands on something that would resonate, he would bite his lip and begin tapping upon the object, using it as a substitute for the tabla and bayan. A hard-bound book, if available, usually suited his purpose very well. He was absent-minded, lost in his moods; it was impossible to distinguish his workdays from his holidays.

The evening concert would draw to a close. I was always wide awake at night. When everyone went to bed, I would roam about, like a follower of the Brahmadaitya. The entire place would be silent and absolutely still.

In the moonlight, the rows of plants on the terrace cast their shadow, tracing the alpana of my dreams in patterns on the floor. Beyond the terrace, the top of the young tree swayed in the breeze, its leaves sparkling in the radiance. I don't know why, but what drew my gaze most insistently was the low attic with a sloping roof, on the terrace of the sleepy house across the alley. Standing there, it seemed to point at something. The night would advance: one o'clock, then two. From the main road in front came the chant of a funeral procession: 'Bolo Hari! Haribol!'

11

Those days, in every home, people fancied keeping birds. Most distressing of all was the call of a caged koel from some house in the neighbourhood. Bouthakrun had acquired a Chinese cuckoo. Its shrill song rose like a fountain from beneath the cloth that shrouded its cage. There were other birds of many varieties, their cages suspended in the southern veranda. Every morning, a worm-seller would provide the birds with their feed. From his bag, he would produce grasshoppers, and sattu for the birds fed on barley.

Jyotidada would answer all my arguments. But one could not expect the same from women. Once, upon a whim,

Bouthakrun kept squirrels in a cage. I told her she was being unjust. She ordered me to stop acting like a gurumoshai or schoolmaster. This was no answer to my argument. So, instead of engaging in a war of words, I found myself compelled to release the two creatures in secret. I had to face some remonstrations after that, but I offered no reply.

There was one thing we regularly quarrelled about—a quarrel that was never resolved. Let me tell you about it:

Umesh was a clever man. At a throwaway price, from the English tailors' shops, he would buy fragments of silk in many hues, and combine them with scraps of net and cheap lace to create ladies' dresses. He would undo the paper wrapping and carefully unfold the dresses before the eyes of his female clients. Behold the latest fashion! he would declare. The women could not resist the enchantment of that magic spell. How deeply it upset me, I cannot describe. I would repeatedly object, in great agitation. Act your age: no need to behave as if you're my uncle!—would be the reply. I pointed out to Bouthakrun that the old-fashioned white, black-bordered sari or the Dhakai sari would be better options, more civilized by far. Don't the deors of today have anything to say about the spectacle of the georgette-wrapped, painted, doll-like appearance of their boudis? Bouthakrun, enshrouded in the outfits tailored by Umesh, was better than that, after all. There was not so much artificiality in dress and appearance, those days.

I could never win a debate with Bouthakrun, because she

never countered my arguments. I also lost to her in chess, at which she was an expert.

*

While on the subject of Jyotidada, a few details must be added, to introduce him properly. We must begin our account from a slightly earlier date.

He had to make frequent trips to Shilaidaha, to attend to his responsibilities as landlord or zamindar. Once, he took me along on such a mission. For those times, this was an unconventional act, what people would consider an extreme step. Jyotidada must have conceived this journey from home into the outside world as a sort of mobile lesson. He had realized that my intellect ranged freely in the sky and open air, drawing sustenance naturally, from the environment. Later, when I had moved up to a higher grade in the school of life, I would mature into an adult in this very place, Shilaidaha.

The old indigo factory still remained. The river Padma was far away. The courthouse was on the ground floor, and on the upper storey, our lodgings. In front was a huge terrace, and beyond it, some enormous jhau, tamarisk trees, that had flourished in tandem with the white indigo planter's trade, once upon a time. Today, in place of the rampant power of the indigo-trading sahib, utter stillness reigns. Where has he gone, the dewan from the indigo factory who was like a messenger from hell! Where is the band of soldiers with belted waists and staves on their shoulders! Where has it gone, the hall with the long banquet table, where the sahibs would enter, riding up from the front door, turning night into day with all their feasting and the whirl of ballroom dancing, their blood bubbling with the intoxication of champagne! The piteous cries of the hapless ryots would not reach the ears of their masters, whose power extended all the way to the district jail. Today, none of this holds true; the only surviving facts from the past are the graves of two sahibs. The tall tamarisks sway in the breeze, and the grandchildren of those old-time peasants sometimes glimpse the sahibs' ghosts wandering in the abandoned garden of the indigo factory in the dead of night.

There I remained, in a solitary frame of mind. I stayed in a small room in the corner, my hours of leisure stretching to fill the vast expanse of the open terrace. This vacation in a different, unfamiliar place was like the dark water of an ancient pond, its depth impossible to plumb. I heard the ceaseless call of the bou-kotha-kau, the Indian nightingale, and a succession of stray thoughts drifted through my mind. Meanwhile, the pages of my notebook had begun to fill with poems. Like the early mango blossom, ready to scatter before the first crop in the month of Magh, those poems have fallen away.

Those days, if a young boy—or especially a girl—set a couple of lines to metre and rhyme, the wise men of the nation would hail it as an unprecedented event, a wonder never to be repeated. I know the names of those maiden poets; their works have appeared in print, as well. Then, as the fashion for expressing nice thoughts in carefully measured fourteen-syllable awkwardly-rhymed lines declined, their names were erased and at once replaced by row upon row of names, belonging to the girls of today.

Boys are far more timid than girls, and much shier. I don't remember any young male writer who composed poems, then, save me alone. One day, a nephew older than me pointed out that words, if cast in a fourteen-syllable mould, assume the shape of a poem. I witnessed this magic myself. In my hands, the fourteen-syllable frame blossomed like a lotus; it even attracted the amorous bee. I had crossed the gulf that separated me from the poets, and I have continued to bridge that gap, ever since.

I remember, when I was studying in the class junior to the year for scholarships, the superintendent, Mr Gobinda, heard it rumoured that I wrote poetry. Imagining that I would bring glory to the name of Normal School, he ordered me to compose verse. I had to write, and recite, for my classmates. I had to hear them remark that the poem was surely plagiarized. The fault-finders did not guess the truth, when later, with maturity, I became an expert at stealing ideas. But then, such stolen goods are precious things.

I remember combining the payar and tripadi or fourteen-syllable and classical metres to compose a poem, expressing the grief I felt when, as I swam to pluck a lotus blossom, the movement of my arms made waves that constantly pushed the lotus away, beyond my reach. Akshay Babu took me to his relatives' home and made them listen to this poem. The boy has a flair for poetry, the relatives declared.

Bouthakrun's behaviour was entirely contrary. She would never acknowledge that I might become a writer, some day. I could never write like Bihari Chakrabarti, she would always say, just to taunt me. I would think dejectedly that had I even merited a much lower rank than he, she could not have so lightly dismissed her young deor's distate for women's love for clothes.

*

Jyotidada was fond of riding. He was even known to have placed Bouthakrun on horseback, to take her down the road to Chitpur for an outing in the Eden Gardens. At Shilaidaha, he gave me a pony. The creature was quite frisky. He dispatched me to take the pony for a run on the Rathatola field. I would take the pony through its paces on that uneven terrain, clinging to its back for dear life. Because Jyotidada staunchly believed that I would not fall, I managed to avoid being unsaddled. Later, he even took me riding on the Kolkata streets. It was no pony this time, but quite a moody horse. One day, with me in the saddle, it raced through the portico, straight to the courtyard where it used to receive its feed of grain. The next day, we parted company.

I have already informed the reader that Jyotidada had mastered the art of rifle shooting. In his heart, he longed to hunt tigers. One day, hunter Biswanath informed us that a tiger had been sighted in the forests of Shilaidaha. Immediately, Jyotidada cocked his rifle and prepared himself for the hunt. Surprisingly, he took me along, as if the likelihood of a crisis had not occurred to him at all.

Biswanath was a practiced hunter, indeed. He knew there was no bravery in shooting at tigers from the machaan, the platform created high up on a tree. He would call out to the tiger, confront the animal, and then shoot. He had never missed his aim.

The woods were dense. In the shadows of such a thick jungle, it was hard to spot a tiger. They notched a sturdy bamboo tree to create a makeshift ladder. Jyotidada clambered up, rifle in hand. My feet were unshod: if a tiger gave me chase, I could not even have retaliated with my shoes. Biswanath signalled to us. For a long time, Jyotidada could not detect anything. As he peered into the bushes, a single tiger stripe at last caught the attention of his bespectacled eyes. He fired. The bullet chanced to hit the tiger's spine. The tiger collapsed, unable to get back onto its feet. Tail thrashing, teeth convulsively gnashing at the twigs within reach, it began to roar very loudly. When I think about the incident, I feel rather suspicious. As far as I know, a tiger doesn't wait so long to die. Its diet the previous night hadn't been craftily laced with opium, had it? Why was it so drowsy, after all?

There was another occasion when a tiger visited the jungles of Shilaidaha. The two of us, brothers together, mounted an elephant and set out in search of the animal. Off went the elephant, its back heaving like an earthquake as it advanced with stately gait, chewing upon the sugar cane it uprooted effortlessly from the fields along the way. The forest

71

confronted us. Pushing with its knees, pulling with its trunk, the elephant began to uproot the trees and fling them down on the ground. We had already heard the stories told by Biswanath's brother Chamru, about the disasters that occur when the tiger jumps on to the elephant's back and digs its claws in. The elephant then rushes through the forest, trumpeting wildly, and the people on its back are smashed, limbs, head and all, against the tree trunks along the way. On that day, as we rode the elephant, that image of crushed bones remained uppermost in our minds. I concealed my terror out of embarrassment, glancing all about me in apparent indifference, as if I was just waiting to attack the tiger, the moment I set my eyes upon it. The elephant entered the depths of the forest. At one point, it stopped in its tracks. The mahout made no attempt to goad it further. Of the two hunting animals, he had greater faith in the tiger. It must have been his greatest fear that Jyotidada would injure the tiger and render it desperate. Suddenly, like a sudden thunderstorm unleashed by the clouds, the tiger lunged forward from the depths of the undergrowth. Our eyes, accustomed to cats, dogs and foxes, were unprepared for the sight of this creature, its massive, arched neck so virile, yet seeming somehow so weightless. Through the open fields it ran, in the glare of the midday sun. What an exquisite, natural gait! The fields were bare of crops. That huge, yellow expanse, bathed in sunshine was the right place, indeed, to gaze one's fill at this vision of a tiger on the run.

There remains an entertaining anecdote to be told. In

Shilaidaha, the gardener would pluck flowers and arrange them in vases. It occurred to me that I could inscribe my verse in the coloured sap of flowers. The fluid I managed to squeeze out with much effort would hardly rise to the nib of the pen. I began to think of creating a machine. A perforated wooden bowl and above it, a rotating pestle, were all that one required. It could be operated with a rope-bound wheel. I informed Jyotidada of my needs. He may have been secretly amused, but outwardly, it was impossible to tell. At his bidding, along came the carpenter with his bits of wood. The machine was constructed. Much as I churned the flower-filled wooden bowl with the rope-bound pestle, the blossoms were crushed to a muddy paste, but no juice flowed from them. Jyotidada realized that flower sap would not rhyme with machine-applied pressure. But still, he did not mock me openly.

In my whole life, this was my only venture at engineering. They say in the scriptures that there is a deity always waiting to humiliate the one who presumes to become what he is not. On this occasion, the same divinity had looked askance at my engineering project. I have stopped handling machinery ever since, avoiding even the stringing of instruments like the sitar and the esraaj.

I have recounted elsewhere how Jyotidada went bankrupt trying to run a fleet of indigenous ships in the rivers of Bengal, in competition with the flotilla companies. Before that happened, Bouthakrun had already left us. Jyotidada had abandoned his abode on the second floor. Ultimately, he built a house on a hill in Ranchi.

12

Now began a new act in the drama of the second-floor room, altering my life.

I had led a gypsy existence once, taking refuge here and there, in the granary, the palki or the empty room on the second-floor terrace. With the arrival of Bouthakrun, a garden sprouted outside the terrace room. A piano appeared in that room upstairs, and fountains of melody began to play, in myriad new tunes.

On the eastern side, in the shade of the attic, Jyotidada's morning coffee would be served. That was when he would read aloud from the first draft of some new play. Sometimes,

I would be called upon to add the odd line of verse in my raw, amateurish style. Gradually, the sunlight would advance, and from the terrace above, we would hear the cawing of crows that were eyeing our pieces of bread. By ten, the shade would vanish, and the terrace would grow hot.

In the afternoon, Jyotidada would go down to the courthouse. Bouthakrun would arrange pieces of fruit, peeled and sliced, on a small silver dish. Adding some sweets she had prepared herself, she would garnish the dish with rose petals. Coconut water, fruit juice, or ice-chilled tender coconut pulp, would be served in a glass. The entire menu for a snack, placed on a small Moradabadi tray called a khunche and covered with a flowered silken napkin, would be dispatched to the courthouse at one or two in the afternoon.

That was when *Bangadarshan* was at the height of its popularity. Bankim's characters, Suryamukhi and Kundanandini, had become a byword in every home, almost like family visitors. Their past, their future, was a matter of anxiety for the entire populace.

When an issue of *Bangadarshan* appeared, the entire neighbourhood stayed up all afternoon. Because of my talent for reading aloud I was conveniently spared the need to snatch and grab. Instead of reading on her own, Bouthakrun preferred to have me read to her. There were no electric fans then; as I read, I would claim my share of the cool breeze stirred up by Bouthakrun's hand-held fan.

13

For a change of air, Jyotidada would sometimes visit the garden estate on the Ganga shore. At that time the riverbank had not yet lost its purity through contact with foreign traders. The birds' nests along the riverside had not withered away, and iron machines with chimneys like elephant trunks had not released their dark breath into the brightness of the sky.

I remember our first sojourn on the shores of the Ganga, in that small, two-storeyed house. It had just begun to rain. The shadow of the clouds floated upon the river current, undulating with the waves; the shadow hung heavy above the forests on the opposite shore. Often, on such a day, I would compose a song of my own. But that day I was reminded of Vidyapati's verse:

In this month of Bhadar, heavy with rain-clouds,
How empty is the temple of my heart!

Setting the words to a tune I had composed, a tune with a classical touch, I made those lines my own. Enamelled with melody, that cloudy day on the Ganga shore survives, even now, in the jewel casket of my rain songs. I remember the gusts of wind that assailed the treetops every now and then, causing a great stirring and swaying among the branches, the dinghies scudding along the river, their white sails tilting in the wind, the splash of tall, plunging waves upon the ghat. When Bouthakrun returned, I sang the song for her. She listened in silence, without uttering a word of praise. I was sixteen or seventeen, then. We still argued about the pettiest of things, but our exchanges had lost their sharpness.

Shortly afterwards, we moved to the garden estate belonging to Moran sahib. It was a virtual palace. The rooms, with ceilings of varying heights, had stained-glass windows, the floor was tiled with marble, a flight of steps rose directly from the riverbank, up to the long veranda. There, I would remain awake all night in a sort of trance, pacing up and down, my steps matching the rhythm of my walk along the Sabarmati river, at another time. That garden estate no longer exists; it has been chewed up and swallowed by the iron teeth of the Dandi factory.

Speaking of the Moran garden estate, I recall the times when meals were cooked in the shade of the bakul tree. The food was not spicy, but it had the magic of an expert touch. I remember, when my brother and I had our poite, the sacred thread ceremony for young Brahmins, Bouthakrun prepared our habishyanna, the ritual meal of boiled rice with ghee made from cow's milk. For those three days, the taste and fragrance of that rice held our greedy minds captive.

I had a major problem: my body rarely succumbed to illness. The other boys in the family, who knew the art of falling sick, would benefit from Bouthakrun's personal care. They not only received her ministrations, but also took up all her time. I would lose my share of her attention.

Then those days on the second floor faded away, taking her along with them. After that, I took up residence on the second floor, but my account of that period cannot blend seamlessly with what had gone before.

*

Our meanderings have brought us to the threshold of my life as a young man. But I must return to the boundaries of my boyhood.

An account of my sixteenth year is required. The beginning of that year had witnessed the emergence of *Bharati*. Nowadays, there is a surge in the publication of journals, everywhere in this region. In retrospect, remembering those crazy days, I understand the headiness of such intoxication. Even a boy like me, with neither learning nor skill, found a place in that gathering without attracting undue notice; clearly, we were caught up in a whirlwind of childishness. The only professional journal to appear in the region those days was *Bangadarshan*. This periodical of ours, *Bharati*, was of uneven quality. The contributions of Borodada, my eldest brother, were difficult to write and as hard to comprehend. To add to that, I produced a story, weaving together delirious ravings I was too young to substantiate, ravings that others, too, were not perceptive enough to analyse, it seems.

This is my cue to speak of Borodada. Jyotidada held court in the second-floor room, and Borodada in the southern veranda. At one stage, he immersed himself absent-mindedly in heavy philosophical ideas beyond our comprehension. His writings and opinions drew a scant audience; he was reluctant to release a willing captive if he found one, or perhaps the person in question would be reluctant to leave him, claiming more from him than philosophical discourse alone. Borodada had acquired a companion of unknown name, universally addressed as 'Philosopher'. The other dadas, my elder brothers, would deride not only his weakness for mutton chops, but also his daily urgent needs of diverse kinds. Apart from philosophy, Borodada enjoyed inventing mathematical problems. Pages full of numerical calculations would flutter about the veranda in the southern breeze. Although Borodada could not sing, he played the Western flute—but this was not for the sake of music, only to measure by calculation the melodic content of various classical ragas and raginis. Then, one day, he started working on *Swapnaprayan*. He started out by creating metrical forms, measuring the sounds of Sanskrit on the weighing scales of Bengali phonetics, and arranging them accordingly. Some he kept and others he discarded, scattering them about in torn scraps of paper. Then he took to writing long verse compositions, casting off much more than what he retained. What he wrote did not easily win his own approval. We lacked the wits to collect and preserve all those lines that he tossed away. As he wrote, he recited; listeners would gather all around him. All of us at home were carried away by the elixir of poetry. While reading aloud, he would sometimes burst into a guffaw. His laughter would fill the skies; carried away by merriment, he would slap the backs of those within reach, driving them to distraction.

That southern veranda was one of the life springs of the Jorasanko House. Eventually, its stream ran dry; Borodada left for the ashram at Shantiniketan. All I remember, sometimes, is the nostalgic autumnal sunshine of the Sharat season, scattered across the garden in front of that veranda as I rendered the song I had just composed:

In the autumn sunshine, as I dream at dawn today,
I know not what my heart yearns for.

I also recall a song from a scorching, blazing afternoon:

All day long, without a care,
What game is this I play with myself?

Borodada had another remarkable habit, and that was his prowess at swimming. Entering the pond, he would swim fifty laps, at the very least. At the Peneti garden estate, he would cross the Ganga and swim a long distance. Taking our cue from him, we too learnt how to swim when we were very young. I had started learning on my own. Soaking my pyjamas, I stretched them wide to fill them with air. As soon as I entered the water, the pyjamas would billow around my middle like a waistband filled with air. Now there was no chance of my drowning. As an adult, while living on the sandbank at Shilaidaha, I once swam across the Padma. The feat was not as awe-inspiring as it may sound. There were times when the Padma, its sandbanks exposed by receding waters, lacked a current forceful enough to command respect. All the same, the story was worth recounting to people onshore, and I have told it many times over. In my childhood, when I visited the Dalhousie hills, my father never forbade my solitary wanderings. Armed with a spiked walking stick, I would clamber from hilltop to hilltop along the walking tracks. Most thrilling, then, were the terrors I conjured up in my own imagination. One day, walking downhill, I had stepped on a heap of dry leaves beneath a tree. When my foot slipped slightly, I immediately steadied myself with the stick. But I may not have recovered my balance, after all. It would have taken no time at all for me to roll down the sloping hillside, into the torrent of the waterfall. I regaled my mother with a highly exaggerated account of what might have happened. Why, while wandering among the dense pinewoods, I might even have chanced upon a bear! That, too, was a tale worth telling. Because nothing eventful had actually taken place, I had conjured up such disasters in my imagination. The story of how I crossed the Padma is not very different from all these tales.

When I entered my seventeenth year, I had to move away from the editorial meetings of *Bharati*.

*

My trip to England was decided upon at this juncture. It was also suggested that, before boarding ship, I should spend time with Mejdada, the second of my elder brothers, to learn the rudiments of Western manners and behaviour. He was then a practising judge in Ahmedabad. His wife—my Mejobouthakrun—and their children were in England, waiting for Mejdada to join them on furlough.

I was uprooted, transplanted from one field to another. Now began the process of coming to terms with my new surroundings. I was too shy to question everything at the very outset. I worried about maintaining my dignity when introduced to total strangers. In an unfamiliar world that was hard to mingle with but impossible to escape, a boy of my temperament constantly came up against emotional stumbling blocks.

In Ahmedabad, my mind flitted about in a scenario drawn from ancient history. The judge's residence was at Shahibagh, in a palace dating back to the Mughal era. In the daytime, Mejdada would be away at work. I would wander all day like one possessed, in the yawning spaces of the enormous empty rooms. From the chatal, the large paved platform in front, one could see the river Sabarmati, its knee-deep waters winding through the sands. In places, embedded in the paving of the water tanks sunk into the chatal, one found imaginary traces of the royal luxuries enjoyed by the begums at their bath.

Brought up in Kolkata, we had never glimpsed the eminence of history. Our short-sighted gaze was trained on the dwarf-like stature of recent times. In Ahmedabad, I found for the first time that the current flow of history had been frozen, permitting a nostalgic backward glance at the aristocratic past. Its ancient past seemed to have been buried underground like some Yaksha's treasure. That was when my imagination received the first intimations of an idea for the story called 'The Hungry Stone' ...

It happened hundreds of years ago. In the nahabatkhana, the enclosure above the guard house, shehnai players with their accompanists performed round the clock, rendering the raginis, classical compositions, appropriate for each period of the day. The street resounded with the rhythmic beat of horses' hooves, as the Turkish cavalry marched by, sunlight flashing from their spearheads. Deadly whispered conspiracies surrounded the emperor's court. Armed with naked swords, Abyssinian eunuchs guarded the private quarters. Fountains of rose water played in the begums' bath or hammam, and the tinkle of armlets and bangles could be heard.

But now, Shahibagh stood still and frozen, like a forgotten story; those colours and sounds were nowhere to be found, the days were dry, the nights drained of all spirit.

The bones of ancient history had been laid bare, the skull had survived, but not the crown. It would be an exaggeration to claim that I had fleshed out the figure, clothing the skeleton in mask and shroud inside the museum of my mind. Having created a backdrop for the idol, I had merely constructed a rough image in my mind, a plaything of my own fancy. Because I remember little and forget a great deal, it becomes easy for me to cobble together this sort of creation. My own image as it appears to me today, after a gap of eighty years, does not correspond to reality in every detail; much of it is a figment of my imagination.

After I had spent some time in this place, it occurred to Mejdada that my heart might find solace in exile if I were introduced to young women who could bring the flavour of the homeland into my life in a foreign country. It would also be an easy way for me to learn the English language. So I stayed for a while with a family in Bombay. One of the daughters of that family, an educated girl of our times, had returned from a trip to England with her learning brilliantly polished. My own knowledge was so limited, she could justifiably have treated me with contempt. But she did not. Lacking a fund of textbook knowledge to impress her with, I never lost an opportunity to inform her of my flair for poetry. That was my most potent strategy for winning respect. The person to whom I had announced my poetic vocation had accepted my claims without weighing or evaluating them. She asked me to call her by a special poetic name, and approved the name that I supplied. She expressed a desire that I cast her name in rhyme. I wove it into a garland of verse, and she heard the name in song, set to the classical tune of Bhairavi. 'O Poet!' she exclaimed. 'Your song would give me renewed life, I think, even on my dying day.'

Clearly, when women wish to express their admiration for someone, they speak of him in terms of honeyed overstatement, with the aim of spreading joy. I remember, it was from her lips that I first heard words of praise for my appearance. Such compliments sometimes revealed great expertise. Once, for instance, she had specially exhorted me: 'You must keep one request of mine. Never grow a beard; let the contours of your countenance never be concealed.'

As everyone knows only too well, I have not yet complied with her wish. Before my disobedience manifested itself upon my countenance, she had passed away.

There were years when birds from foreign climes would suddenly come to nest in that banyan tree of ours. By the time one learned to recognize the dance of their wings, they would have flown away. From distant forests they would come, bringing with them their unfamiliar songs. So, sometimes, in the course of our life's journey, come messengers of our soulmates from unknown parts of the world, to enlarge the kingdoms of our hearts. They arrive unbidden. But there comes a time, one day, when they no longer answer to our call. Departing, they edge our life's fabric with an embroidery of flowers, leaving our days and nights forever enriched.

14

The sculptor who created me began his handiwork with Bengali clay. The rough contours of an initial likeness took shape. That was my childhood, made of pure stuff with few admixtures. Most of its ingredients were stored up within my own self, while some other elements were determined by the atmosphere and the people at home. Often, the process of character building stops at this point. Those who also undergo the special treatment of being pounded into shape in the education factory acquire the distinctive market value of a brand name.

By a quirk of fate, I had almost managed to evade that

factory. All the tutors and pundits specially deployed to train me had despaired of my ever completing my education. Mr Gyanchandra Bhattacharya, son of Mr Anandachandra Vedantabagish, was a graduate. He had realized that a boy like me could not be forced to tread the beaten path of learning. The problem was, the wise men of the time had not sufficiently emphasized the essential need to cast all boys in the mould of the genteel bhadralok graduate. Those days, there was no urge to haul everyone, rich or poor, into the same dragnet of college education. As our family then had eminence but no wealth, this trend had continued. Their concern for education was rather slack. At one stage, when we reached the pre-scholarship level, we were transferred to DeCruz Sahib's Bengal Academy. It was our guardians' hope that we would acquire a respectable measure of expertise in English conversation, if nothing else. In the Latin class, I was deaf-and-dumb; all my exercise books remained blank from beginning to end, the pages white as a widow's garb. The teacher had complained to DeCruz Sahib about my extraordinary stubbornness in not doing my work. DeCruz had explained to him that we were not born to study: we had entered this world for the sole purpose of paying our monthly fees. Gyan babu had also arrived at a somewhat similar conclusion. But even in this situation, he had found a way. He made me learn *Kumarasambhava* by heart, from beginning to end. He locked me into my room, to ensure I mastered *Macbeth*. Meanwhile, Pundit Ramasarvasya taught me *Shakuntala*. He allowed me to stray beyond the boundaries of classroom study, and this proved fruitful, to an extent. These were the ingredients that went into the making of my mind, when I was a boy. There were also Bengali books of all kinds, freely and indiscriminately available.

*

I moved to England where the process of character formation began to acquire the stamp of foreign craftsmanship, a procedure known in chemistry as the production of a compound substance. I detect here the hand of fate: I had gone there to glean some learning in the customary way, but despite some effort, these plans did not materialize. Mejobouthakrun was there, and so were her children. I remained entangled in the net of family affairs. I hovered on the fringes of school culture; home tutors were engaged, but I shirked my work. The little knowledge I gained was from human intimacy. In a variety of ways, the English environment worked upon my mind.

Palit sahib weaned me away from my bondage to the family. I took up lodgings in a doctor's house. They made me forget I had arrived in a foreign land. Mrs Scott's affection for me was utterly pure. She always showed a maternal concern for my well-being. I was then a student at London University, where Henry Morley taught us English Literature. This was not the dry stuff of textbooks. In his mind, in the timbre of his voice, literature would come to life, touching us in that corner of our heart where the soul seeks succour.

Nothing of the flavour would be lost in transmission. Returning home, I would flip through the books published by Clarendon Press, to familiarize myself with their contents. In other words, I had assumed the task of tutoring myself.

From time to time, Mrs Scott would feel that my health was fading. She would grow agitated. She did not know that my body had closed its gates to illness, ever since I was a child. Every day, I would bathe at dawn in ice-cold water. In the medical opinion of the times, to survive in such a lawless state amounted to heresy.

I could spend only three months at the university. But my foreign education was almost entirely the product of human intercourse. Our Sculptor takes every opportunity to add new elements to His creation. During those three months, my intimacy with the English heart had produced such a mingling of elements. I had been assigned the task of reciting instalments of verse, drama or history every evening, until eleven. In that short time, I read a great deal. Such reading did not belong to the classroom. It was a union of literature and the human heart.

I went to England, but did not become a barrister. I encountered no experience violent enough to shake the early foundations of my life. I absorbed within myself the fusion of East and West. In my own heart, I discovered the meaning of my name.*

*[Note: Tagore's name 'Robi', means 'sun', which does not distinguish East from West.]

Translator's Note

*B*oyhood Days, or *Chhelebela*, as it was called in the Bengali, is a sequence of reminiscences spanning the period from Rabindranath Tagore's earliest memories to the time of his first visit to England in 1878. Urged by litterateur Nityanandabinod Goswami to write something for his students at Shantiniketan, Tagore tells us in his Preface that he thought of trying to recapture the aura of his young days. Tagore probably began writing *Chhelebela* as a prose poem during his stay at Mangpu in April 1940. Manuscripts at Rabindrabhavan in Shantiniketan include two poems that bear out this idea: 'Palki' ('The Palanquin', dated 24 April 1940), which closely resembles the beginning of chapter 2 and the end of chapter 6 of *Chhelebela*, and 'Balyadasha' ('The State of Infancy', 28 April 1940), which anticipates the end of chapter 7. *Chhelebela* was published some time in August–September 1940 (Bhadra 1347, according to the Bengali calendar).

An English translation by Marjorie Sykes, titled *My Boyhood Days*, was serialized in the *Vishwa Bharati Quarterly* in 1940 and published as a book by Vishwa Bharati, Kolkata, in the same year. More recently, some brief extracts from *Chhelebela*, translated by Suvro Chatterjee, have been included in the section titled *My Childhood* in *Selected Writings for Children* (Oxford, 2002), edited by Sukanta Chaudhuri. Marjorie Sykes' translation has some significant omissions. 'The Boy', a poem from an earlier collection, *Chhorar Chhobi* (1937), included in the original Bengali text of *Chhelebela*, does not figure in Sykes' edition. Neither does Tagore's own Preface. These framing texts enhance our understanding and appreciation of the main work, and their absence in the translated version is a loss to the reader. The extracts in the Oxford anthology focus on the early sections without highlighting the important later chapters of *Chhelebela*, which trace the maturing consciousness of a young adolescent awakening to his role as a writer and his interest in women.

The present translation is an attempt to approach the text of *Chhelebela* in its entirety. Tagore's Preface as well as the poem 'The Boy', have been included. While choosing an idiom suitable for younger readers of today, I have also tried to preserve the flavour of the particular ethos that the original text seeks to recapture. Many Bengali terms have been retained. Where the context does not make their meaning clear, supplementary information has been provided in the last section of this book. In many instances, names have been spelled according to their Bengali originals and Anglicized spellings have been dropped. Most translations from Bengali, including Sykes' *My Boyhood Days*, use English terms such as 'brother', 'aunt', 'brother-in-law' and 'sister-in-law', which do not adequately capture the intricacies of Bengali family relationships. In this translation, words such as 'dada', 'didi', 'deor' and 'khuri' have been used, with a brief explanation where necessary, to preserve the specificity of these kinship terms. Bengali words referring to food, clothing and items of daily life have also been retained where possible, for they are vital to the atmosphere of Tagore's text.

The structure of *Chhelebela* is whimsical and episodic. Tagore recollects his childhood through vivid descriptions and colourful anecdotes interspersed with musings and reflections upon the past. The memories he recounts are often linked to one another by association of ideas rather than by chronology. Many of the persons, places and episodes described here figure in the earlier text *Jibonsmriti* (*My Reminiscences,* 1912) which Tagore describes as a series of 'memory pictures' that reveal the story of his inner life. But the sense of wonder and mystery that suffuses the world of *Boyhood Days* is missing from *My Reminiscences*. There are no ghosts in the earlier account, but in *Chhelebela*, the irrational and the supernatural lurk around every corner and the child's fantasy world is as real to him as his external social environment. Biographers point out Tagore's departures from factual truth in his emotional recollection of the past in *Boyhood Days*. The Tagore mansion in Jorasanko, for instance, actually consisted of two houses, one occupied by Debendranath's family and the other by the descendants of his younger brother, but the text makes no precise distinction between the two houses, suggesting a fluid interaction and close-knit atmosphere within the extended family. This harmonious image is not quite consistent, though, with Tagore's representations of family life in his other writings. In *Boyhood Days*, Tagore emphasizes the austerity of his upbringing and the lack of proper clothing, but family records show that a considerable amount was spent on socks, shoes and kurtas for the young Robi between 1865 and 1868. Some readers feel that this imagined lack of clothes was Tagore's way of signifying the absence of affection and warmth in his childhood home.

A fabric woven of personal memory, the text is also a testament to a bygone age. A whole social milieu, an entire way of life, is presented impressionistically through a child's eye perspective. The simplicity of the past becomes a touchstone for judging the complexities of the present, just as the magical realm of childhood becomes a measure of the loss of imagination that growing up entails.

Yet the world of Tagore's remembered boyhood remains far from idyllic. The silences in the narrative are as significant as the details that are recounted. Dark experiences, the pain of loss, the tensions of life within a joint family, are passed over lightly. If nostalgia for the past is one of the text's dominant emotions, what also resonates poignantly is the loneliness of the young boy Robi, the disjunction between his outer world and inner life, his freedom of spirit and resistance to educational straitjackets, and his longing for love and companionship. The language of *Chhelebela* is simple and colloquial, expressing a childlike vision. But, especially in the later chapters, it often masks feelings and attitudes that are more mature.

Many of the emotions that were to haunt Tagore's later writings have their roots in this period of his life: a strong affinity with nature, solitariness, a wistful yearning for love, a passion for music, a wide-ranging, curious mind, and an urge to transform the mundane into the extraordinary. The ruins of the Shahibagh Palace in Ahmedabad fired his imagination, generating the idea for his famous story 'The Hungry Stone'. A rainy day beside the river or a sunny autumn afternoon on the veranda would inspire some of his best-known songs. For *Chhelebela* is not only the story of a boy's journey to adulthood and an epitaph to a bygone age but also an account of a writer's awakening to his vocation.

I must acknowledge here the contribution of a few people associated with this project. I am deeply honoured that Amartya Sen has consented to write the Introduction. I am grateful to Sayoni Basu for her involvement in the initial stages and to Sudeshna Shome Ghosh for her painstaking scrutiny of the manuscript and her valuable suggestions. Meena Bhat's supplementary notes at the end should be a bonus for young readers. Above all, I appreciate the support of my family, without whose patience and encouragement this book could not have been written.

Translating *Chhelebela* has been a process full of excitement and despair. For while this translation aims to revive interest in an important literary work by making it accessible to a new generation of readers in the twenty-first century, it also strives to remind these readers of the original text's rootedness in a particular time and place. Today's reader must approach *Chhelebela* at two removes, distanced in time from the world of 1940 when a mature Tagore wrote his reminiscences, and even more so from the late-nineteenth-century scenario of the poet's remembered childhood. Those who do not read Bengali are also distanced from the language and culture of the original text. To bridge these divides, to accomplish a modern translation that also preserves an old-world atmosphere, has proved a double-edged, almost insurmountable challenge. All the same, if it succeeds in bringing a generation of young readers closer to the remembered life, emotions and early experiences of one of the literary giants of our world, this translation can fulfil an important purpose.

New Delhi   Radha Chakravarty
September 2006

Radha Chakravarty teaches literature at Gargi College, University of Delhi. Her translations include *Crossings: Stories from Bangladesh and India*, *Chokher Bali*, *Farewell Song: Shesher Kabita*, *In the Name of the Mother: Four Stories by Mahasweta Devi* and *Kapalkundala*. She has also compiled and edited *Bodymaps: Stories by South Asian Women Writers*. She was nominated for the Crossword Translation Award 2004.

PUFFIN  CLASSICS

Boyhood Days

CONTENTS

BORN: Tuesday, 7 May 1861
LOCATION: Jorasanko House, 6, Dwarakanath Thakur Lane, Kolkata
MARRIED: At the age of twenty-two to Bhabatarini Debi, whose name was changed to Mrinalini Debi after marriage
CHILDREN: Five, three of whom predeceased him
TRAVELS: England, the whole of the Indian subcontinent, the United States of America, Europe, Canada, Russia, South America, Burma (Myanmar), Singapore, Hong Kong, Japan and China
HONOURS AND AWARDS: 1913—Nobel Prize for Literature
1915—D.Litt. from University of Calcutta
1915—Received a Knighthood from King George V of Great Britain
1940—D.Litt. from the University of Oxford, England
DIED: 7 August 1941

Where was he educated?

He tried several conventional schools but found it difficult to conform to the restricted syllabus. Eventually he had numerous home tutors. He was sent to England in 1878 to study to become a barrister, but returned within two years.

What was his family background?

Tagore was born into an eminent family. He was the ninth son of Debendranath Tagore and Sarada Debi. His grandfather, Dwarakanath Tagore, was a zamindar and also a social reformer. Debendranath Tagore was a leading member of the Brahmo

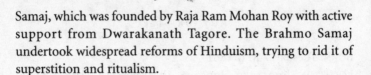

Samaj, which was founded by Raja Ram Mohan Roy with active support from Dwarakanath Tagore. The Brahmo Samaj undertook widespread reforms of Hinduism, trying to rid it of superstition and ritualism.

About this book

In this book, the author recollects his childhood days and compares them to the present, giving the reader a panoramic view of his early life. Though the youthful Tagore is the focus of the story, he also offers glimpses of people, situations and incidents that shaped his thinking. Many episodes narrated here also appear in Tagore's memoirs *Jibonsmriti*.

What was Tagore's contribution to Indian literature and the arts?

His unconventional education allowed full rein to Tagore's versatile talents. Jorasanko House (Tagore House) published two magazines regularly, the *Bharati* and the *Balak*, and his literary skills were honed by regular contributions to them. His first book of poems, *Kabi Kahini* (*The Tale of a Poet*) was published in 1878. The year 1880 saw the publication of two musical plays, followed by *Sandhya Sangeet* (*Evening Songs*) in 1882. It is said that the book so impressed Bankimchandra Chatterjee that he took off the garland from his own neck at a function and put it around Tagore's. In 1890, Tagore went to supervise the family estates in Shilaidaha. There, in 1909, deeply influenced by his natural surroundings, he began writing *Gitanjali*, which he completed in 1911. In 1912, the English translation of *Gitanjali*, with an introduction by William Butler Yeats and a cover sketch by noted painter William Rothenstein, was published in England.

A prolific writer of novels, plays, short stories and essays, he also created a new form of music called Rabindra sangeet.

He composed the national anthems of two countries . . .

In 1911, Tagore composed *Jana gana mana*, the national anthem of India, and in 1971, Bangladesh adopted for its national anthem Tagore's *Amar sonar Bangla*.

And contributed greatly to India's freedom movement . . .

* At the 1890 session of the Indian National Congress, he sang *Vande mataram*, which went on to become India's national song.
* He protested against the partition of Bengal in 1905 and introduced Rakhi bandhan, when Hindus and Muslims asserted their brotherhood and the unity of Bengal by tying the traditional symbolic thread on each other's wrists.
* In 1919, he wrote a letter to Lord Chelmsford, repudiating his knighthood in protest against the massacre at Jallianwala Bagh in Amritsar, Punjab.

How was the university at Shantiniketan born?

Tagore's father Debendranath had founded an ashram at Shantiniketan in 1863. In 1901, Tagore founded a school here (originally called Bolpur Brahmacharyashram) patterned on the ancient gurukul/ashram system of education in India. Its mission was to blend the traditional ashram method of teaching with Western education. He wanted to combine simple living with the appreciation of beauty. Instead of four walls, lessons in Shantiniketan were held in the open, under trees. He started the school with five pupils and five teachers, three of whom were

Christians. It eventually came to be known as the Vishwabharati University in 1921.

Shantiniketan made an immense contribution to the revival of Indian art, culture and philosophy. Many famous people graduated from Shantiniketan, Satyajit Ray and Indira Gandhi among them.

Did Tagore have an influence on other world figures?

Yes! He carried on a lengthy correspondence with Leo Tolstoy and had several meetings with Albert Einstein where they discussed a wide range of subjects. The Argentine poet Victoria Ocampo appeared as a character in one of his books. And he had debates with Mahatma Gandhi on the place of India in the world.

How was Gitanjali *received when it was published, first in Bengali, then English?*

Tagore started writing the poems when he was in Shilaidaha, in 1909. Now in Bangladesh, the village is situated at the confluence of the rivers Padma and Gorai. The land in the area belonged to the Tagore family. He translated the poems into English. By 1912 they were ready for publication. The India Society, an association of Indophiles, people who were involved in promoting knowledge about India, published the book in London. *Gitanjali* created a sensation in the English literary world on publication.

In the Bengali version, he moved away from the earlier archaic literary form and introduced a whole new manner of expression, blending the colloquial and the poetic.

Today, his entire body of writing remains as inspiring as when they first appeared.

THE MYTH OF NARASIMHA AND HIRANYAKASHIPU

The story of Hiranyakashipu appears in the *Bhagwad Purana*. Hiranyakashipu and his brother Hiranyaksha were both rakshasas. Hiranyaksha was killed by Vishnu when he appeared in his Varaha (boar) avatar. Hiranyakashipu vowed vengeance and practised penance to gain magical powers from Brahma. Hiranyakashipu asked for the book of immortality which Brahma declined to give him. Then Hiranyakashipu asked that he should die neither from natural causes nor by means of a weapon; neither on land, in space, by fire or water; neither during the day or night; neither inside the house or outside; and be killed by neither a human, a god or an animal.

It was forbidden to worship Vishnu in Hiranyakashipu's kingdom, but his son, Prahlad, was a staunch devotee and refused to stop worshipping him. Hiranyakashipu tried to eliminate him in many ways—by poisoning him, drowning him, commanding elephants to trample him—all to no avail. He even made his sister, Holika, sit in the middle of a fire with Prahlad in her lap; Holika got burnt but Prahlad was saved once again by Vishnu. Finally Hiranyakashipu ordered an iron pillar to be heated and asked Prahlad to embrace it. As he did so, a miracle happened. The pillar burst open and Vishnu in his Narasimha (half man, half lion) avatar emerged. Vishnu seized Hiranyakashipu and took him to the threshold of his palace. Narasimha was neither man nor animal, and the time was twilight, neither day nor night. Narasimha laid Hiranyakashipu across his thighs (neither on land nor in space) and tore him open with his claws. Thus Hiranyakashipu was killed while abiding by the boon granted to him. And Prahlad came to symbolize true faith in god.

THE ZAMINDARI SYSTEM

'Zamindar' is a Persian word meaning 'holder of real estate'. The zamindari system came into existence in India during the seventeenth century when the power of the Mughals was in decline. Zamindars were appointed to collect taxes from peasants. They did not own the land.

This practice was continued by the British for the collection of revenue. However, the zamindar became synonymous with 'landlord' after 1793. The zamindar would collect revenue from the peasants and hand over the collected taxes to the British authorities, keeping back a portion for himself. The zamindars styled themselves as 'rajas' and lived on the estates in large spacious mansions. They maintained a lavish lifestyle and supported the British during the 1857 Mutiny and also in the early years of the independence movement. Few of them cared for the plight of their peasants, and some of them were content to be absentee landlords, which increased the suffering of the peasants since they had no one to turn to for succour.

The system was abolished in India and East Pakistan (now Bangladesh) after independence, but it is still current in Pakistan in the areas of Punjab and Sind.

THE ANDAMAN ISLANDS

At the end of the Sepoy Mutiny or First War of Independence in 1857, the British exiled those mutineers whom they did not kill, to a group of islands in the Bay of Bengal. The Andaman and

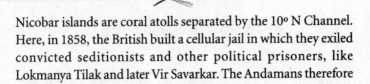

Nicobar islands are coral atolls separated by the 10° N Channel. Here, in 1858, the British built a cellular jail in which they exiled convicted seditionists and other political prisoners, like Lokmanya Tilak and later Vir Savarkar. The Andamans therefore symbolized exile.

Some things to do:

1. Compare the lifestyle of a zamindari household like Tagore's with that of a wealthy household of today.
2. Tagore vividly describes some of his childhood games. Do you think these would be interesting to the modern child? What games do you like to play?
3. Compare Tagore's mother's attitude to education with that of present-day parents.
4. Draw a palki or palanquin after looking it up in the encyclopaedia or on the internet. Also read a poem by Sarojini Naidu called 'The Palanquin Bearers' which will give you an idea of the use of the palanquin. Do you think this might be an ideal vehicle in which a child could set out on an imaginary journey?
5. Shantiniketan symbolizes a fusion of Indian and Western ideas, of the ancient and the modern systems of education. Can you name an educational institution in your city that operates along similar lines?
6. Tagore corresponded with many famous men. Imagine you are reading his letters to Tolstoy, Einstein, Yeats and Mahatma Gandhi. What could be the topics for these letters or conversations? Write out a dialogue between Tagore and one of them, ensuring that the character of each person is brought out clearly.

WHO'S WHO IN *BOYHOOD DAYS*

(In order of appearance)

Goswamiji: Nityanandabinod Goswami, literary scholar and teacher at Shantiniketan

our tutor, Mastermoshai: Aghornath Chattopadhyay, a medical scholar, who tutored Tagore, along with his elder brother Somendranath and his nephew Satyaprasad Gangopadhyay, from 1869

my grandfather: Dwarakanath Tagore (1794–1846)

my grandmother: Digambari Debi (?–1839)

Sejdada: Hemendranath Tagore (1844–84)

my mother: Sarada Debi (1828–75)

Doctor Nilmadhab: Nilmadhab Haldar, the Tagores' family physician since 1866

Kishori Chatujje: Kishorinath Chattopadhyay, a follower of Maharshi Debendranath and a folk-musician who taught Tagore many songs

khuri: Shubhankari Debi

my brother-in-law: Saradaprasad Gangopadhyay, married to Tagore's elder sister Soudamini Debi

Mejokaka: Girindranath Tagore (1820–54)

Sejdada was busy grooming his daughter: Hemendranath's daughter was Protibha Debi (1865–1922). She was removed from Bethune School and admitted to Loreto House in 1879.

Bishnu: Bishnuchandra Chakrabarti (1819–1901); he was appointed a Brahmo Samaj singer by Raja Ram Mohan Roy in 1830, to convey the Brahmo philosophy through his music

Srikantha babu: Srikanthasingha, Debendranath's friend

Jadubhatta: Jadunath Bhattacharya (1840–83), a famous musician

Ramprasad Sen: an eighteenth-century musician famous for his lyrics in praise of Goddess Kali

Kana Pehelwan: the blind wrestler was called Hira Singh

Tutor Nilkamal: Nilkamal Ghoshal, who began tutoring Tagore in 1866

Sitanath Dutta: Tagore's teacher, he was actually named Sitanath Ghosh. He was interested in medical cures and technical innovations.

my gymnastics trainer: Shyamacharan Ghosh, a well-known gymnast

Boudidi/Bouthakrun: Usually refers to Jyotirindranath Tagore's wife Kadambari Debi (1859–84). She married Jyotirindranath Tagore on 13 July 1868. Kadambari Debi committed suicide on 19 April 1884. In places, this term also refers to Satyendranath

Tagore's wife Gyanadanandini Debi (1850–1941).

my father: Maharshi Debendranath Tagore (1817–1905); well-known essayist and a leading member of the Brahmo Samaj

Jyotidada: Jyotirindranath Tagore (1849–1925); well-known playwright and composer

Mejdada: Satyendranath Tagore (1842–1923); the first Indian to join the Indian Civil Service

Akshay Chowdhury: a famous poet (1850–98), whose writings influenced Tagore; a close friend of Jyotirindranath

Moran sahib: Indigo merchant Moran had built a huge and expensive mansion at Gondalpara in Chandannagar, which the Tagores visited in 1881 (approximate date)

Borodada: Dwijendranath Tagore (1840–1926)

my Mejobouthakrun and their children: Gyanadanandini Debi, Surendranath Tagore and Indira Debi

a family in Bombay: the family of Dr Atmaram Pandurang

an educated girl: Anna, as Annapurna Tarkhad was known. Tagore gave her 'a special poetic name' of Nalini. Anna died in 1891.

Anandachandra Vedantabagish: a leading member of the Brahmo Samaj

Pundit Ramasarvasya: Ramasarvasya Vidyabhushan Bhattacharya

Palit sahib: Taraknath Palit, who set up the Society for Promotion of Technological Education in Bengal (SPTE) in 1906

Henry Morley: a well-known professor of English literature who taught at University College London from 1865 to 1889

FAMILY RELATIONSHIPS IN BENGALI

Father	Baba
Mother	Ma
Daughter	Meye
Son	Chheley
Older sister	Didi
Younger sister	Chhoto bone
Older brother	Dada
Younger brother	Chhoto bhai
Middle brother	Mejo dada (Mejda)
Sister-in-law (elder brother's wife)	Boudidi/Bouthakrun
Brother-in-law (husband's younger brother)	Deor
Paternal aunt (wife of father's younger brother)	Khuri

GLOSSARY

Airavat: sacred elephant belonging to Indra, king of gods in Hindu mythology

alaap: the introductory part of a composition in Indian classical music

albola: a hookah with a long, flexible smoking tube

aloo dum: a potato dish

alpana: traditional designs painted on the floor for rituals and auspicious occasions

alta: red lac-dye used by Bengali women to paint the borders of their feet

amburi: tobacco perfumed with ambergris

bakul: a flower, *mimusops elengi*

Bolo Hari! Haribol!: the chanting of Krishna's name by pall-bearers on the way to a cremation

Bangadarshan: journal edited by Bankimchandra Chatterjee. The first issue appeared in April 1872.

Bangadhipa Parajaya: 'The Defeat of the Rulers of Bengal' (1869, 1884) in two volumes, by Pratapchandra Ghosh. It recounts the struggle between Pratapaditya, who ruled Bengal from 1560 to 1610, and the Mughals, who ultimately vanquished him.

bankh: a yoke slung over the shoulder to carry loads suspended from both ends

bari: pigeon-pea paste dried in small conical shapes, and used in cooking

Baroan: a melodic mode in Indian classical music

belphul: Arabian jasmine, *jasminum sambac*

Bhadar: Bhadra, fifth month of the Bengali calendar, mid-August to mid-September

Bharati: a journal launched in 1877. Dwijendranath Tagore was the first editor.

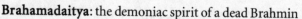

Brahamadaitya: the demoniac spirit of a dead Brahmin

Chaitra: last month of Bengali calendar, from mid-March to mid-April

chameli: fragrant flower, *jasminum grandiflorum*

Chanakya: Kautilya, minister of Chandragupta Maurya (4th century BC) and a great political strategist

chandimandap: pavilion for worship of Durga, open on one side

chemise: a long, loose dress

dhunuri: a person who cleans cotton by shredding it with a bow or cotton-gin

dolonchampa: a type of flower

dugdugi: small tabor

esraaj: a stringed musical instrument played with a bow

First Book of Pyari Sarkar: Pyaricharan Sarkar's *First Book of Reading* (1850)

gamchha: a handwoven napkin or towel

gandharaj: a fragrant flower, *gardenia jasminoides*

ghat: landing stage on the banks of a river or pond

ghoti: a small pot

goja: a type of sweetmeat made of flour

golap-paash: a vessel with perforated nozzle for spraying rose water

gurguri: a hookah with a long flexible tube

habishyanna: boiled sunned rice and ghee, served to those observing a ritual fast

handi: a clay pot

'The Hungry Stone': famous story by Tagore, published in the journal *Sadhana*

jatra: traditional popular opera or theatre in Bengal, usually performed in the open

jhama: a piece of over-burnt brick used to scrub the body

kalboishakhi: Nor'wester, afternoon storm that commonly occurs in April and May in Bengal and other parts of eastern India

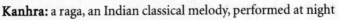

Kanhra: a raga, an Indian classical melody, performed at night

karabi: a flower, *nerium indicum*

Kartik: seventh month in the Bengali calendar, from mid-October to mid-November

Krittivasa: fifteenth-century Bengali poet Krittivasa Ojha, author of the popular Bengali Ramayana

kulin: a Brahmin of pure caste, much in demand in the marriage market. Kulin Brahmins were often married several times, to brides much younger than themselves.

Kumarasambhava: Kalidasa's long Sanskrit poem about the Hindu deities Shiva and Parvati and the birth of their child, Kartikeya. A partial translation by Tagore was published in *Bharati* in 1880.

Kundanandini: a female character in Bankimchandra Chatterjee's novel *Bishabriksha*

luchi: round unleavened bread fried in ghee

mahout: elephant trainer

Meghnadbadh Kabya: an epic poem by Michael Madhusudan Dutt. Meghnad is Ravana's son in the Ramayana.

mourola: a type of tiny, delicious fish

Mugdhabodh: a Sanskrit grammar by Bhopadeva

Narada: a sage known both for his learning and quarrelsomeness

naru: a round sweetmeat usually made of coconut, sugar and molasses

New Market: perhaps a reference to the market formerly called Sir Steward Hogg Market, opened to the public in 1874

Normal School: actually a reference to the Calcutta Government Pathshala or Calcutta Model School, which, after 1860–61, was located in the same building as Normal School, an institution for training teachers established under the supervision of Ishwarchandra Vidyasagar in 1855

Padma: a river in eastern Bengal

pakur: a kind of fig tree, *ficus infectoria*

panchali: musical theatrical performances in Bengali popular culture

pathshala: a primary school

payar: verse composed in fourteen-syllable lines

Pharashdanga: a place in Bengal famous for its fine weaves

Peneti garden: Ashutosh Deb's riverside garden estate at Peneti, where some members of the Tagore family went in 1872, to escape the dengue epidemic in Kolkata

raga: a melodic mode in Hindustani classical music

Ragini Bihag: a melody in Hindustani classical music

revri: a sweetmeat made of sesame cooked in sugar or molasses

Rijupath: a Sanskrit reader compiled by Ishwarchandra Vidyasagar

Sabarmati: a river in Gujarat; the Shahibagh palace is situated on its banks

sandesh: a type of sweetmeat made of cottage cheese

Shakuntala: famous play by Kalidasa, also the name of the heroine of the play

shloka: a Sanskrit couplet

Shandamarka: Shanda and Amarka, two brothers who taught Prahlad, son of Hiranyakashipu

Sharat: the autumnal season

singara: Bengali version of the samosa, a stuffed savoury snack

Sitar Banabas: 'Sita in Exile' by Ishwarchandra Vidyasagar, based on an episode from the Ramayana

Suryamukhi: a female character in Bankimchandra Chatterjee's novel *Bishabriksha*

Swapnaprayan: a volume of poetry by Dwijendranath Tagore, published in 1875

tabla and bayan: a pair of small percussion instruments in Hindustani classical music

teele-goja: a type of sesame-flavoured sweetmeat

tripadi: poetic metre in Sanskrit and Bengali verse

ustad: trainer; music teacher; a master artist or craftsman

Valmiki: the sage who is supposed to have composed the Ramayana

Vidyapati: Vaishnava poet of the fourteenth century

Yaksha's treasure: underground treasure guarded by a yaksha, a demigod or underworld spirit